The
Power
of
Releasing

TURNING LOOSE
AND LETTING GO

WAYNE KNIFFEN

WESTBOW
PRESS®
A DIVISION OF THOMAS NELSON
& ZONDERVAN

WestBow Press books may be ordered through booksellers or by contacting:

WestBow Press
A Division of Thomas Nelson & Zondervan
1663 Liberty Drive
Bloomington, IN 47403
www.westbowpress.com
844-714-3454

Scripture quotations marked NKJV are taken from the New King James Version.
Copyright © 1982 by Thomas Nelson, Inc. Used by permission. All rights reserved.

Scripture quotations marked NLT are taken from the Holy Bible,
New Living Translation, copyright © 1996, 2004, 2015 by Tyndale
House Foundation. Used by permission of Tyndale House Publishers,
Inc., Carol Stream, Illinois 60188. All rights reserved.

ISBN: 978-1-6642-9958-0 (sc)
ISBN: 978-1-6642-9959-7 (hc)
ISBN: 978-1-6642-9960-3 (e)

Library of Congress Control Number: 2023908678

Print information available on the last page.

WestBow Press rev. date: 5/12/2023

Contents

Foreword

"Just let it go." "Leave it at the feet of Jesus." "Lay it down at the cross and move on." I would venture to say that every one of us have heard things like this said in an attempt to help someone get through a difficult season. Most of the time, people who give this type of counsel are well-intended, but unknowingly they make something that may be very difficult seem like all it takes to make past hurts and pains vanish is to snap our fingers.

Most of us who have given these brief one-liners are sincere and well-meaning. All we want is for people to be healed from their hurts and disappointments; to find peace and have closure. And yet, this kind of guidance has little to no lasting effect. Both the giver and receiver of this type of counsel, walk away still bruised and defeated by the enemy. This is exactly where Satan wants us; controlled and incarcerated by past hurts and experiences.

Through biblical illustrations and personal experiences, my brother explains the power that comes from releasing. He describes how releasing what we are holding on to, can actually set us free. Releasing affords us the opportunity to enjoy the freedom and liberty that we have in Christ. When Jesus sets us free, we are free indeed (John 8:36 NKJV).

The Power of Releasing can be easily read and understood. It would make a great guide for small-group studies, Sunday bible classes; even taught from the pulpit. As Christians, the word of God tells us how to live the abundant life that Jesus made available to all who will believe. It is possible to live in peace with God, ourselves and with those around us, when we experience the power that comes from turning things loose; including people. This book weaves God's word through our daily lives and describes what it looks like to walk in freedom and victory, when we make the hard decision to turn loose of whatever has been dragging us around.

Let me give you a quote from The Power of Releasing. It just may whet your appetite to want more of what this book is offering. "Holding grudges is pointless and exhausting. When we hold a grudge against someone, we are constantly thinking about them and the event that caused our pain. Our emotions stay raw and sensitive. It doesn't take much of a bump to cause us to relive hurtful events. We are the ones who will suffer, not the ones that we refuse to release. Many times, the one we hold resentment toward doesn't even know it. It makes it very difficult to move on in life when we are holding on to the past. We must release in order to increase."

Keith Kniffen
Senior Pastor
Kingdom Living
Cowboy Church
Poynor, Texas

Preface

Releasing can be the most difficult thing we ever do, and sometimes it can be the easiest thing we do. Since everyone is different, the grip we have on things have varying degrees of pressure. Some things are held tightly while other things are held loosely. The tighter we hold on to something, the greater the pain we experience when our fingers are pried loose. Let go and let God may be easy to say, it may look cute on a ball cap, and it may be cool embroidered on a tee shirt, but it can be very difficult to do.

I vividly remember my first water skiing experience. The guys who were giving me instructions were pretty good skiers. They were also full of tomfoolery. It was not uncharacteristic for them to set you up for a "gotcha" moment. Their instructions to me were, "When you fall, whatever you do, don't turn loose of the ski rope". You know where this story is going don't you, especially if you water ski.

Being an individual with strong intestinal fortitude, sometimes to my detriment, I was determined to conquer the sport of water skiing. When the driver of the boat took off, everyone shouted for me to—"hold on"! I grabbed the ski rope handle with a vice-like grip. We did not go very far when I went down head first. I lost both skies but I did not lose my grip on the ski rope handle. The next thing I knew, I was on my way to the bottom of the lake, and going down fast. I came close to losing my bathing suit in the process. The pressure from the water and the pull of the boat caused the rope handle to disengage from my hands. The instant the ski rope released from my hands was when that horrific moment ended. Immediately, I began to return to the surface of the water.

By the time I reached the surface, the boat had circled around to retrieve me. Everyone in the boat was laughing hysterically. They knew what would happen if I did not turn loose of the rope. Now, I know what will happen if you do not release your grip on a ski rope when you fall. You will be pulled to the bottom of the lake. It will not be an enjoyable experience. As long as I held on to the rope, I was at the mercy of my situation. It was not a pleasant one either. Once the rope released from my hands, I could feel the weight and pressure of that terrifying moment lift.

This book is not about the sport of water skiing. I will leave that assignment to someone who is more skilled at the sport than I am. This book is about releasing those things in our lives that keep pulling us under emotionally and spiritually. One of the most dangerous things we can do to our emotional and spiritual health is to keep holding on to what we need to turn loose. As long as we refuse to let go, we will be pulled and jerked around by what we refuse to release. By holding on we will be controlled by the very thing we are trying to control. Turning loose and letting go is a personal choice. It is an act of the will, so choose wisely.

I pray the Lord will use each chapter in this book to help you identify things or people, you need to release and let go. It is the prayer of my heart that by the end of this book, you will be much freer than you were when you started.

The more we are willing to release, the freer we will be to live and enjoy life. It is up to us how long we are pulled around by what we are holding on to. It is time to turn loose and let go. There is power in releasing. The peace every heart longs for is at the tip of our fingers.

> "I want to say thank you to all the people who walked into my life and made it outstanding, and all the people who walked out of my life and made it fantastic."— Unknown

The Power of Releasing
You Have A Miracle
In Your Hand

WHAT DO YOU HAVE IN YOUR HAND? THE ANSWER TO THIS question will depend on who answers it. Someone might say they have a cup of coffee in their hand, others might say they have a Bible or a cell phone, or some may say they have nothing in their hands. Let me ask this question in a different way. What are you holding on to? What is it that you need to let go but you are finding it next to impossible to release? Most of us, if not all of us, maintain a grip on something or on someone that we need to let go.

Let me tell you up front what you have in your hand. You have a miracle. That is right, a miracle. The chances are very good that there is something, or someone, you need to release and allow God to do what only He is capable of doing—performing a miracle. God cannot trust us with what we have not released.

In Exodus 3–4 God was having a conversation with an eighty-year old man. The voice of God was coming through a bush that was on fire, but it was not consumed. The conversation they were having was about

1

deliverance ministry. God told Moses that he had been handpicked to lead the people of God out of Egyptian captivity. I know it is difficult to do, but try to imagine yourself in Moses's sandals. You are having a conversation with a burning bush, and the voice coming from this bush has identified itself as God.

I think it is understandable why Moses responded to this deliverance ministry assignment the way he did. His first response was "I am not your man" (Exodus 3:11 NKJV). When God continued to press Moses about what He wanted him to do, he said, "I cannot be your man" (Exodus 4:10 NKJV). Finally, Moses told God, "I will not be your man" (Exodus 4:13 NKJV). This is what Moses was telling God. In essence he was saying, "God, you have made a mistake. I am not your man. I cannot be your man. Let's keep this real, God; I will not be your man." Just in case you think you can duke it out with God, let me remind you of something. There is a name for the person who wants to go toe-to-toe with God—casualty.

Why was it so hard for Moses to say yes to God? Because he still remembered what put him on the backside of the desert— for forty-years, I might add. It was hard for Moses to let go of what happened to him in Egypt. He was still holding on to all the pain of that moment. Moses tried to free God's people forty years earlier, and in the process, he killed an Egyptian. In Exodus 2, we read about Moses fleeing to the land of Midian in fear for his life. The land of Midian was on the backside of the backside of the wilderness. What put him there? He had given that *delivering the people* business a shot, and it did not work out well. Look at what it had gotten him. Moses could not accept God's assignment, because he could not let go of what happened to him in the past. Who knows, there may be some "wanted dead or alive" posters still floating around in Egypt on him.

Here is a brief glimpse into the life of Moses at this juncture. He had spent forty years living in Pharaoh's house learning how to be a somebody. He spent the next forty years of his life in the wilderness learning how to be a nobody. Now, Moses was being given the opportunity to experience how God can take a nobody and make them somebody—at the age of eighty.

I think the age of Moses at this moment in his life is an important side note. He was eighty years old. God can and will use anyone, regardless of their age, to do great exploits for Him. We are never too old for God to use us for His glory. All He is waiting for from us is, "Here I am, Lord. Send me."

You Have a Miracle in Your Hands

The question we began this chapter with is the same question God asked Moses: "What is that in your hand?" (Exodus 4:2 NKJV). Moses responded by saying, "It is just a simple shepherd's staff." In other words, it was an ordinary stick. Moses was about to learn that God is able to take something that is ordinary and turn it into something that is extraordinary.

Moses was instructed by God to throw the stick to the ground. For that to happen, Moses had to loosen his grip, turn the stick loose, and let it go. When the rod left Moses's hand and hit the ground, a miracle happened. The stick became a serpent, and Moses fled. Fleeing from the serpent was the first wise thing Moses did up to this point.

Let's slow this story down a tad. When did the stick become a snake? When did the miracle of the shepherd's rod becoming a serpent happen? When Moses loosened his grip on the rod and released it. Is it beginning to sink in? Moses had a miracle in his hands all the while, and he did not know it. What are you holding on to? Is there something or someone you need to release and let go? You, too, have a miracle in your hands.

Let me be honest. I would have had a hard time obeying what God told Moses to do next. "Reach out your hand and take it by the tail" (Exodus 4:4 NKJV). I can relate to the fleeing part, but to reach down and pick up the snake? That is a different thing altogether. I'm just thankful this is Moses's story. Moses obeyed God and picked up the snake by its tail. Once it was back in his hands, another miracle happened; the snake became a stick once again.

Here is another principle about the power of releasing. Whatever we turn loose, God will transform it, then place it back into our hands to be used as a testimony to His power and glory. Moses was carrying an ordinary shepherd's staff that had been touched by the power of God (Exodus 4:20 NKJV). It was now called the rod of God, but it was in the hands of Moses. It was by this transformed rod that miracles, signs, and wonders were performed.

Like Mother Like Son

Let's go all the way back to when Moses was born. Even though the Hebrew people were slaves in Egypt, God continued to bless them, and they kept increasing in number. One day it dawned on Pharaoh that if a foreign enemy were to attack, the Hebrew people might rise up and join the invading force and defeat the Egyptians. So he came up with a plan. He instructed all the midwives to perform live-birth abortions on baby boys born to Hebrew women. The girl babies would be spared. Because the midwives feared the Lord, they did not carry out the orders they had been given by Pharaoh. The king got wind of it and summoned all the midwives to the palace. He demanded to know why they had refused to follow his instructions to kill all the baby boys who were being born. They lied and said, "The Hebrew women are not like the Egyptian women. They are strong. By the time we get there, they have already given birth" (Exodus 1:19 NKJV). These midwives were shown favor by God.

Since the king's orders to kill baby boys at birth were not followed, he issued another edict. Every Hebrew son who was born was to be thrown into the Nile River and drowned. During this time frame, a baby boy was born to Amram and Jochebed. They named him Moses. That's right, the same Moses who released the stick that became a snake.

Jochebed was able to safely hide baby Moses for three months. When this was no longer possible, Jochebed was faced with a gut-wrenching decision. "But when she could no longer hide him, she got a basket made of papyrus reeds and water-proofed it with tar and pitch. She put the baby in the basket and laid it among the reeds along the bank of the Nile River" (Exodus 2:3 NKJV). I cannot fathom what must have gone through Jochebed's spirit when she set her baby adrift in the river. Can you imagine how difficult it was for this mother to take her hands off the basket and release her baby into the reeds? If she had not released Moses, the chances are very good he would have died with the other baby boys. Maybe Jochebed should get some of the credit for the Israelites' deliverance from Egyptian captivity. Just saying.

When Jochebed took her hands off the basket and released baby Moses into the river, God went to work. It just happened to be the day when Pharaoh's daughter made her routine trip to the river to bathe. The first thing she saw was the floating basket that baby Moses lay in. She had her maidservant retrieve the basket and the baby from the water. Watching from a vantage point close by was Miriam, the older sister of Moses. I have always wondered if Jochebed had stationed Miriam by the river's edge to watch over her baby brother.

Miriam asked Pharaoh's daughter if she would like for her to go and get one of the Hebrew women to come and nurse the child for her. Miriam was granted permission to do just that, and guess who she got? Jochebed, the mother of baby Moses. "Then Pharaoh's daughter said to her, 'Take this child away and nurse him for me, and I will give you your wages.' So the woman took the child and nursed him" (Exodus 2:9 NKJV). Look at that! Jochebed was able to raise her own son, and she got paid to do it. How good is that? What she released was now back in her arms.

This miracle happened because a mother did the most difficult thing a person can ever do, she released. Once she released her baby boy, God went to work. He performed a miracle and gave her son back to her. She was able to not only raise her son in the home of the enemy, she got paid for doing it. God prepared a table before her in the presence of her enemy (Psalms 23:5 NKJV).

When Moses obeyed God by releasing his rod, God performed a miracle and it became the rod of God: He was doing the same thing his mother did when she released him into the Nile River. Her releasing him led to the release of the Hebrew people from Egyptian captivity.

The Principle of Releasing Is Still in Effect Today

We will never have what we have not released. That can be anything. It can be your business, your children, grandkids, spouse, your marriage, your life, memories, relationships, past hurts, whatever. You can make your own list. Turning loose and letting go is the only way to actually possess what you have.

Several years ago, plans were being finalized for our fiftieth high school graduation celebration. There was a lot of chit-chat going back and forth between former classmates concerning this special event that was drawing close. Even though we had a very special senior class, there were a few individuals who said they would not be participating. When pressed for a reason for not attending this special, once in a lifetime event, I was taken aback a little by the answer I was given. Some were still nursing emotional hurts and pains that went as far back as their junior high days. As I listened to their venting, it became clear that the majority of their hurts did not come from actual events, but from their perception of what happened. Their perception had become their reality. They would not let the past go. My response to them was, there is nothing wrong with an eighteen-year old teenager that fifty-years cannot cure. To my delight, most of them did change their minds and came. A few of them chose not to.

Isn't it amazing that a person can and will allow things that happened as long as fifty-years ago, to drag them around emotionally? After all those years, some people are still nursing wounds that should be scars by now. A scar is a healed wound. Our testimony comes from our scars not our wounds. The older we get, the harder it can be for us to release things. Moses was eighty.

After serving as a pastor for almost fifty-years, I have listened to many people share the painful events and hurts of their past. Some have been very emotional when they shared their story. It is as if the event they are describing just happened. They relive their emotional pain every time they talk about it. It never ceases to amaze me when I find out that what they are talking about happened ten-years ago, fifteen-years ago, and even longer. For some strange reason, they would not or could not let go. If we refuse to let go of something, there may come a time when we cannot let it go. Releasing is a choice and it should be done as quickly as possible.

I was sitting at a table with six people who I knew fairly well. We were attending a mission conference. The conference had not started yet, so the entire room was buzzing with the sound of laughter and small talk. During our casual conversation, someone asked one of the ladies at our table how her elderly mother was doing. What this lady shared taught me so much about the power of releasing.

Her mother had reached the age where she was keenly aware of her mortality, and was giving her material possessions to her kids. The process of giving her belongings away had gone on for about a year. Then a tragic thing happened. Her house caught fire and burned to the ground. Everything she had left was destroyed by the fire. Her adult kids came to her rescue. They offered to give back everything she had given away. What her mother said to them still has a home in my heart to this day. "The only things I have left are the things I have given away." Oh my! Turning loose and letting go can be a challenge, but the truth is, the only things that we really have, are the things we have given away.

The Connecting Link Between
Temptation and Participation

"Blessed *(happy)* is the man Who *walks* not in the counsel of the ungodly, nor *stands* in the path of sinners, nor *sits* in the seat of the scornful" (Psalms 1:1, NKJV; emphasis added). Notice the progression given in this verse. It goes from walking, to standing, to sitting. The connecting link between walking and sitting, is standing. The connecting link between temptation and participation, is hesitation. Hesitation will get you into trouble every time. The connecting link, is holding on to what we need to turn loose.

We see this principle played out in the moral downfall of King David. One evening, while he was walking on the roof top of his house, he saw a beautiful woman named Bathsheba bathing. David looked, he lingered, and he lusted. This was the beginning of a slippery slope for the King. The connecting link between his looking and lusting, was his lingering. His lingering led to adultery and his adultery led to murder. Lingering is holding on to what needs to be turned loose. Holding on to something or to someone that needs to be released can be very costly.

Holding on to or releasing something, is a personal decision that we make out of our free will. If we choose to hold on to what we need to let go, we voluntarily remain a captive. "And Elijah came to all the people, and said, *'How long will you falter between two opinions?* If the Lord is God, follow Him; but if Baal, follow him.' But the people answered him not a word." (1 Kings 18:21, NKJV italics added) The people were lingering, wobbling, between holding on to God and releasing Baal; or holding on to Baal and releasing God. They could not have both.

God cannot trust us with what we have not released. Always keep this in mind when it comes to turning loose of things or people. The tighter the grip that you have on something, the greater the pain will be, when your fingers are pried loose. There is power in releasing. Releasing not only frees us, releasing will keep us free. You have a miracle in your hand.

The Power of Releasing
The Potential of a Little in the Right Hands

THERE ARE ONLY TWO MIRACLES THAT ARE RECORDED IN ALL four of the Gospels. The resurrection and the feeding of the 5,000 men, not including the women and children. I've read accounts that anywhere between 12,000 to 20,000 people might have been fed with this miracle meal of fish and chips. Each Gospel writer shares this same event with slight differences, but there is one common point they all share, "So they all ate and were filled" (Matthew 14:20, NKJV). Not only was there enough food to feed this large crowd, everyone was as able to eat all they wanted, and there were twelve baskets of scraps left over. Maybe the Lord wanted each disciple to have a doggie bag for their upcoming boat ride.

This is an incredible story filled with obscure, yet significant details that can be easily over looked. Jesus had just received word about the death of John the Baptist. When Jesus heard the news, He departed by boat to a remote area to spend some time alone. Sometimes when you receive disturbing news, you just want to have some time by yourself, some time to think and reflect. This was not going to happen. The people heard where Jesus was headed, so they followed after Him on foot. When Jesus arrived at His destination, He saw the huge crowd that had assembled. Moved with compassion, He began to heal their sick and minister to their needs.

Ministering to this huge crowd went on for hours, because all four Gospel writers say, "When it was evening" (Matthew 14:15, NKJV). Jesus' compassion for the people overrode His own need for rest and reflection. Mark says in his account of this story, Jesus saw that the people were like sheep, not having a shepherd. He spent the entire day ministering to the people and teaching them the word of God. Ministering and teaching can be very draining, especially when you do it for an entire day. Jesus forfeited His rest to bring rest to the people.

It appears that it may have been the disciples who became antsy and wanted to bring the day to a conclusion. They approached Jesus and reminded Him that the day was just about spent, and they, along with this huge crowd, were in a deserted place. There was no place for them to buy food. Since night was falling, the crowd needed to be dismissed so the people could go to the surrounding villages to buy food. The disciples probably thought Jesus would agree with their assessment of the situation and bring the meeting to a conclusion. They just knew the next words that came out of Jesus' mouth would be, "Rise for the benediction". That was not what they heard.

"But Jesus said to them, 'They do not need to go away. You give them something to eat'" (Matthew 14:16, NKJV). It sounds to me like Jesus asked His disciples the same question God asked Moses, "What is that in your hand" (Exodus 4:2, NKJV). The disciples had to have been stunned by these words. They were keenly aware of the size of this crowd. I am sure the size of the crowd made their small lunch appear even smaller. The disciples did not have the resources to feed such a large group of people. All they had was five small loaves of bread and two fish. Five biscuits and two fish, is not going to feed one hungry man, much less five-thousand men; not including the women and the children who were there.

The disciples were about to see first-hand that with God a little provision can become more-than-enough when we place it in His hands. When we cannot trace God's hand, we can always trust His heart.

We Get Increase from What We Release

Jesus told His disciples to bring Him the bread and fish. When the bread and fish was released from the hands of the disciples into the hands of Jesus, He blesses it, breaks it and hands it back to His disciples. Pay attention to the process. What the disciples gave to Jesus, He blesses it, and gives it back to them. It is now heaven's bread but it is in the hands of the disciples, just like the rod of God was in the hands of Moses.

This large crowd of people were instructed to sit down in numbered groups. With the blessed bread back in their hands, the disciples began to serve the fish and chip meal. The miracle of the small lunch of five loathes of bread and two fish, becoming more than enough to feed thousands of people, happened in the hands of the disciples. This is a demonstration of the power that is in releasing whatever we are holding on to. Increase comes from what we are willing to release.

I cannot imagine what must have been going through the minds of the disciples as they began to serve this small lunch to this large crowd of people. I can hear them mumbling under their breath something like, "I don't think this is going to work." "This could get embarrassing". "It's going to get ugly." "After these men eat all they want there won't be enough left to feed the women and the children." As they continued to release the limited amount of fish and bread that was in their hands, the increase continued. When it was all said and done, everyone had eaten their fill and there was plenty of leftovers. This is a miracle. They had more food left than they started with. The disciples were holding a miracle in their hands and did not know it until they placed what they had into the hands of Jesus.

Our Giving Sets the Standard for Our Receiving

We determine our own yardstick of measurement for receiving. Let me say this in another way. God allows us to determine the measure by which we receive. What we are willing to release will determine the measure of our increase. Listen to what Jesus said about giving and receiving: "Give, and you will receive. Your gift will return to you in full—pressed down, shaken together to make room for more, running over, and poured into your lap. The amount you give will determine the amount you get back" (Luke 6:38 NLT). God allows us to determine the measure by which we receive. Jesus said that the amount we give will determine the amount we get.

Most of the teaching that we hear today on this passage of scripture is about stewardship when it should be about Lordship. To understand the principle of releasing and receiving we must leave Luke 6:38 in its context. In verse 27 Jesus talks about loving our enemies and doing good to those who hate us. He is not talking about a national enemy in this passage. He is talking about our personal enemies. In verse 28 we are to pray for those who have hurt us. Jesus says that we are to help those who cannot or will not return the favor. Then He talks about not judging people and being quick to forgive. That is the context of Luke 6:38. The measure by which we release love, good deeds, forgiveness, judgement, etc., determines how much of these things we receive. God uses our giving as the measuring stick by which we receive. The amount we give will determine the amount we get back. Jesus is literally saying that God's provision is in our hands.

It's Not Always Easy to Turn Loose and Let Go

All of my friends are well aware that I am a computer whiz. Well, maybe not. When I see a computer, I get that deer in the headlight look. I cannot tell you why but computers and technology as a whole, intimidate me. This is weird too because I use a computer every day.

Back in the early 80's some men in my church told me that I

needed to catch up with twentieth-century technology and buy a computer. I was perfectly content with doing what I did by hand, and I was very reluctant to listen to their counsel. It was not long after this conversation about my need for a computer, these guys brought one to my office and gave it to me. One of the men had updated his computer system and was giving me his old one. They were thrilled now that their pastor had a computer. I was intimidated from the get-go even though it was a very simple system.

It took several months but I slowly began to enjoy my new computer. I was still overawed by it but I was finding it to be very beneficial. I even thought, how in the world did I ever get along without one. Every week I would be asked by some of the men who had given me the computer, how I liked it. My response would be something like, "I'm getting more and more comfortable with it." About a year later they came to me with a proposal. Actually, it was not a proposal at all, it was a demand. A man in our church had surrendered to the ministry and had enrolled in college to pursue his education. The guys told me that they were giving my computer to him because he needed one for his college studies. That is right, they did not ask me, they told me what they were going to do. I bet you cannot guess what I was thinking?

Put yourself in my shoes. I'm just now getting over being intimidated by my new computer and the men who gave it to me are telling me they are giving it to someone else. How dare them. Being their pastor, I could not tell them what I really thought. How in the world could I say no to their request? How would that make me look? If a pastor ever blows it with a parishioner, the chances are nil-next-to-none they will ever get a change to renegotiate with them. So, I bit my tongue and held my peace. I'm just thankful they could not hear what I was thinking. Did you know that it is possible to think in color?

A couple of months after these men had confiscated my computer, my secretary buzzed me on my phone and said that some of our men were there to see me. It was the same group that had reneged on their computer gift. When I opened the door of my office, they were all smiles. In their hands was a brand-new computer system that was far better and more sophisticated than the one they had given me earlier. I was so thankful that I did not tell them what I was thinking when they came and took back the computer, they had given me earlier. What I received was so much better than what I had released, even though I had a bad attitude in the process.

These men knew all along what they were going to do when they told me they wanted to take back the gift they had given to me and give it to someone else. Don't you think our heavenly Father knows what He is going to do if we will release whatever we have in our hands? He is all knowing. What we get from Him will be so much better than what we released to Him.

We can never over-estimate the power of releasing. What we release has the potential to come back to us, pressed down shaken together, and running over.

Little Things Can Make A Big Difference When Released

Have you noticed that when God chooses to do something big, He will usually use someone or something that is small? We see this over and over again from Genesis to Revelation. When Paul wrote his first letter to the church at Corinth, he reminded them that oftentimes God chooses things that the world considers foolish for the purpose of shaming those who think they are wise. He chooses and uses things that are weak to shame those who think they are strong. Sometimes God will choose those things that the world thinks are unimportant to bring to nowt what the world thinks is necessary. This way no one can boast about their exploits.

A Handful of Flour and A Little Oil

In the book of 1 Kings, we have a very intriguing story about the Prophet Elijah and his encounter with a widow lady who was destitute. When Elijah saw her, she was in the process of gathering some sticks to build a fire, so she and her son could have their last meal before they died. "So he (Elijah) went to Zarephath. As he arrived at the gates of the village, he saw a widow gathering sticks, and he asked her, 'Would you please bring me a little water in a cup?' As she was going to get it, he called to her, 'Bring me a bite of bread, too'" (1 Kings 17:10–11 NLT). Did Elijah not know this woman's condition? He should have. He is a prophet for crying out loud. Her immediate response was, "I don't have a single piece of bread in the house. And I have only a handful of flour left in the jar and a little cooking oil in the bottom of the jug. I was just gathering a few sticks to cook this last meal, and then my son and I will die (1 Kings 17:12 NLT). Elijah knew her condition. He was not being insensitive to her needs. He was giving her the opportunity to see how God can take whatever we have in our hands, no matter how small, and use it to supply all of our needs.

Elijah told her to continue what she was doing but to make him a small piece of bread first. Then, she could use what was left of the flour and oil to prepare a meal for herself and for her son. The woman was obedient to do what the prophet had asked of her—"So she did as Elijah said, and she and Elijah and her family continued to eat for many days. There was always enough flour and olive oil left in the containers, just as the Lord had promised through Elijah (1 Kings 17:15–16 NLT). The miracle that she needed to sustain her life was in her hands all the while. As long as she kept releasing the flour and the oil that she had, there was plenty to eat. Her supply kept coming back to her, pressed down, shaken together, and running over. As long as she kept releasing her little, there was plenty.

A Small Rock Took Out A Big Problem

In 1 Samuel we have the story of David facing a huge problem and all he had in his hand was a small rock. Everyone knows that you do not take on a giant with just a stone. That is ludicrous. Goliath thought it was too—"Come to me, and I will give your flesh to the birds of the air and the beasts of the field" (1 Samuel 17:44 NKJV). David knew something that Goliath did not know, but he was about to find out. God can use something that the world considers weak to take out something that seems to be strong. God can use something that seems foolish to confound the wise. When this happens, only God can get the glory. It was not the stone that David used that took out the giant. It was the name of the Lord: "I come to you in the name of the Lord of hosts" (1 Samuel 17:45 NKJV).

"So David triumphed over the Philistine with only a sling and a stone, for he had no sword" (1 Samuel 17:50 NLT). God used the stone to take out the giant when David released it. It is amazing what God can do with what we have in our hands when we are willing to turn it loose. When it is in our hands it is limited and seems to be insignificant. In His hands it becomes unlimited and incredibly significant.

A Sling and A Prayer

What giant(s) are you facing? Does the deck seem like it is stacked against you? Does your situation appear to be hopeless? The question becomes, what do you have in your hands? Instead of having a wing and a prayer, maybe all you need is a sling and a prayer. You will find that to be more than enough.

Sometimes prayer may seem to be the least thing you can do, when actually it is the most that you can do. Release your voice unto the Lord. "Don't worry about anything; instead, pray about everything. Tell God what you need, and thank him for all he has done. Then you will experience God's peace, which exceeds anything we can understand. His peace will guard your hearts and minds as you live in Christ" (Philippians 4:6–7 NLT). Talk to God about everything.

Always keep in mind that prayer is not a monologue; prayer is a dialogue. Praying is having a conversation with your heavenly Father. In a healthy conversation both parties talk and both parties listen. That means we need to spend just as much time listening (if not more) to God, as we do when we are talking to God. God knows everything about everything and has promised to teach us all things (John 14:26 NKJV). It would be wise on our part to spend some time listening to what He has to say about what we are talking to Him about.

When was the last time you had a serious conversation with the Lord? If you can remember what you said to Him but you cannot remember what He said to you, did you really pray. You gave a monologue but you did not have dialogue with Him. Prayer is a two-way conversation. Prayer is the provision you will always have in your hands. All you need is a sling and a prayer.

The Power of Releasing
The First Peter Principle

You may have heard the expression, "Don't saddle me with your problems"? When someone says that, what do they mean, what are they actually saying? They are saying that they do not want you to burden them with what is bothering you. Keep your issues to yourself. Leave them out of your private business. When I was growing up in East Texas, country folks would say it this way; "Every tub must sit on its own bottom." That is a way of saying, "You take care of your issues and I will take care of mine". Every person is responsible for taking care of their own problems. It is your problem, you fix it.

If we embrace this kind of mindset about how we deal with problems, and most of us have, we will find it very difficult to follow what I call the First Peter Principle—casting all of our worries and fears on the Lord. After all, we do not want to bother the Lord with all of the stuff that is weighing us down. So, we will just take the 'big things', the things that we cannot handle to the Lord, and we will decide what is big and what is not.

"Casting all your care upon Him, for He cares for you" (1 Peter 5:7 NKJV). Have you noticed that this is not a complete sentence?

This verse begins with a present participle, casting. The word casting, functioning as an adjective, connects us to the previous verse. "Therefore, *humble yourselves* under the mighty hand of God, that He may exalt you in due time" (1 Peter 5:6 NKJ emphasis added). How do we humble ourselves? By casting all of our worries on God. If we are not saddling God with our worries, then we are not walking in true humility. We humble ourselves when we depend on God's grace for our lives.

Most Christians are like the hitchhiker who could not solicit a ride. They were weary and exhausted from walking for hours carrying their heavy bag on their shoulder. Finally, an individual driving a pickup truck pulls over and offers them a ride. The fatigued hitchhiker laboriously climbs into the bed of the pickup and the driver returns to the highway. When the driver looks in their rearview mirror, they see the hitchhiker standing in the back of the pickup with their heavy bag still on their shoulder. Even though the hitchhiker now has the opportunity to rest and relax, they choose not to, by standing and refusing to put down their heavy bag. The vehicle has the ability to provide the rest they desperately needed and were looking for, but they did not take advantage of their opportunity.

This is a classic illustration of how a lot of Christians manage their burdens. Even though we are in Christ, who is more than capable of relieving us of our weariness, we choose to hang on to our burdens and worries, instead of releasing them to His care.

Worry Is Nothing More Than Fear in Disguise

Fear and trust are opposites. Trusting God is the antidote to fear and worry. Our big issue is, we are not sure about the last five words of verse 7: "For He (God) cares for you." This is where the rubber meets the road. If we are not convinced that God really cares for us, then we will find it difficult to relax and find our rest in Him. We will become spiritual hitchhikers. We may be in Christ, but we will keep holding on to our heavy burdens. After all, it is our cross to bear. Every tub must sit on its own bottom.

When you cast all of your worries upon the Lord, He exchanges your fear for His peace. It is not the will of the Father for His children to continuously live under the weight of their burdens. When you find yourself under pressure from worry, you need to stop, take a deep breath, and relax in God's grace. He really does care for you.

We humble ourselves before God by casting all of our cares on Him, not just some of our cares. Releasing our worries and fears to God is how we humble ourselves. This is the First Peter Principle.

How do we cast our anxious distractions on the Lord? By trusting that He really cares for us. You cannot carry your burdens and cast them on the Lord at the same time. When we turn loose and let go, all of our anxious distractions will be swallowed up by our trust in our loving Father. The weight from our fears and worries will shift from our shoulders to His shoulders.

Fear Can Be A Friend

Fear can be a powerful emotion that triggers our awareness of just how much we need God, so that we run to Him. Fear can be a friend. The Lord never told us that we should never feel fear. He told us not to be afraid. Fear is an emotion, being afraid is a condition. The phrase "fear not" is mentioned roughly 365 times in the bible. Fear not is the most repeated command in the entire scriptures. "Those who fear the Lord are secure; he will be a refuge for their children" (Proverbs 14:26 NLT). The fear of the Lord is our strength and our sanctuary.

In September of 1997 my son called to tell me what he wanted for his twenty-first birthday. The conversation went something like this: "Hey dad, I know what I want for my birthday. I want to go skydiving with you." You can imagine how taken aback I was at his request. My son is turning twenty-one and I am approaching the half-century mark. I have not jumped since I was an invincible nineteen-year-old paratrooper in the military. I had never skydived. In the military we made static line jumps. The deployment of the main canopy of our parachute was initiated by a static line that was attached to the aircraft. The altitude of our jump usually took place at around 3,600 feet, not at the altitude of 8,000 to 10,000 feet skydivers jump from.

Even though I had a little apprehension about my son's idea, I set out to make it happen. After all, how often do you get to skydive with your son? In a town close to where we lived, there was a small airport that had a skydiving school. They had several packages that you could purchase to make your adventure memorable. I picked the most elaborate one they had. The package I chose, not only included our jump, we also had a photographer who would go with us to video our experience. Once we returned to the hanger, we would watch the video, then we could choose the music we wanted for the background of our video. Our experience of skydiving on my son's twenty-first birthday would be documented and preserved for posterity.

It is jump day! For several hours we spent time preparing for our jump by watching videos, listening to our instructors talk about safety procedures, getting familiar with our equipment, and things we should do and things we should not do. As you can imagine, everyone was very attentive.

Because it had been a long time since I had jumped, the instructors would not let me go solo. They said that I had to be tethered to an instructor. I gave the impression that I was disappointed by not being allowed to jump by myself, but deep down inside I was saying, "Thank you Jesus, thank you Jesus!" I did not want my son to think his dad had lost his spunk or his mettle.

There was not an ounce of anxiety in me whatsoever throughout the entire instruction period, or when the small plane lifted off the ground. Everyone on board was enjoying the moment, giving each other high-fives, thumbs up, checking video equipment, and just making the moment memorable.

When the plane reached an altitude of 8,600 feet, the pilot feathered the engine. That was the first time my stomach turned over during this whole experience. Reality was sinking in. When one of the camera men slid the door of the plane open, fear rushed in. I had flashbacks. I know what can happen when you jump out of a perfectly good flying airplane. I have seen it firsthand. Before I could take my next breath, the man who was taking the video had climbed out on the wing of the plane and was nodding for us to get ready. The instructor that I was strapped to, began to nudge me to the open door. When we got to the door, he said in a loud voice, (so I could hear over the rush of wind that was coming through the door of the plane), "When you feel me push, turn loose of both sides of the door. Remember, we will make our roll and when we come up, go into a spread eagle." No sooner had he said that, the firm push came. It felt more like a shove than a push. Out the door went this fifty-year old man attached to his jump instructor.

Yes, I am not going to lie. I felt fear, but I was determined not to be afraid. How was that possible? I followed the Frist Peter Principle. I humbled myself by placing my trust in the seasoned instructor that I was attached to. He had the experience and was more than capable of taking care of me. He was going to do everything within his power to make sure I was safe and protected. By casting my anxious distraction on my instructor and trusting in his ability to take care of me, I was able to relax and enjoy our trip back to the ground. My son enjoyed his jump experience too. We both still have our videos that document that incredible birthday memory.

God will use fear to draw us to Himself. Since we are in Christ, we might as well relax and trust in His ability to care for us no matter what life may throw at us. This is why it is important to release our fears to Him. We can trust that His word is true. He does care for us. Fear can be our friend. It is okay to feel fear, just don't be afraid.

I love the acrostic of fear that was shared with me years ago by an old pastor friend: False—Evidence—Appearing—Real.

"But when I am afraid, I will put my trust in you. I
praise God for what he has promised. I trust in God,
so why should I be afraid? What can mere mortals do
to me" (Psalms 56:3–4 NLT)?

Fear Can Be A Foe

Fear can be a crippling emotion that triggers a flight response,
so that we run from God. Fear can be a formable foe. The spirit of
fear did not enter the human race until after the fall of humanity.
"Then the Lord God called to Adam and said to him, 'Where are
you?' So he said, 'I heard Your voice in the garden and I was afraid
because I was naked; and I hid myself'" (Genesis 3:9–10 NKJV).
Adam is fearful so he is running, he is hiding from God. This is the
first mention of fear.

Fear is a bully that will try to fill you with insecurities, hurt, and
self-doubt. Its goal is to manipulate and control you. Fear that is not
confronted with the truth can create panic and cause us to make ill-
advised decisions. The enemy wants to use fear to drive us away from
God, to question God's trustworthiness. When we are assaulted by
fear, can we really trust that God cares for us?

"For God has not given us a spirit of fear, but of power and of
love and of a sound mind" (2 Timothy 1:7 NKJV). This verse does
not say that God has not given us *the spirit* of fear. It says that God
has not given us *a spirit* of fear. A spirit of fear is demonic. When we
allow *a spirit of fear* to bully us, we cannot walk in what God has given
us. We cannot operate in the power of God, we cannot love, without
manipulating others, and we cannot have healthy thoughts. A spirit of
fear will kill, steal, and destroy. We know from John 10:10 who's job
description that belongs to.

For several months I was being constantly attacked by a tormenting
spirit of fear. This spirit of fear kept telling me that I was going to die,
and even had the audacity to name the date of my demise. This was

not my first time to grapple with a spirit of fear, but the difference this time was in how unrelenting and vicious this assault was.

The biggest mistake that I made was keeping it to myself. I did not tell a soul and I know better. As long as we keep things in the dark the enemy can wreak havoc. Exposure is the devil's kryptonite. He is a liar and the father of all lies (John 8:44 NKJV). He hates the truth because there is no truth in him. Rudyard Kipling was spot on when he said, "Of all the liars in the world, sometimes the worst are our own fears."

This spirit of fear started affecting my ability to concentrate for any length of time. It was beginning to rob me of the abundant life that I have as a new creation in Christ. A spirit of fear is a thief and it has no scruples. Fear can certainly be a formable foe but, "He who is in you is greater than he who is in the world" (1 John 4:4 NKJV). The enemy of fear is no match for the child of God who knows their identity in Christ.

The day came when I finally had enough. While driving down the street, I yelled as loud as I possibly could, "Spirit of fear, I rebuke you in the name of Jesus. I am a child of God and you have no authority over me. I command you to cease and desist your lying attack—now! In the name of Jesus, you leave and take all your imps with you." I rolled down the window of my pickup truck and spit as hard as I could. The spirit of fear left immediately and has not returned. To some that may sound a little drastic or over-the-top. Well, sometimes that is what it takes to break free from the foe of fear. Desperate times call for desperate measures. I am just thankful that no one who knows me witnessed it. Then again, someone may have, but they have never said anything.

The strategy of a spirit of fear is to block us from all of our birthright privileges as children of God. I love what Jack Cranfield (author of Chicken Soup for the Soul) says about fear. "Everything you want is on the other side of fear." The enemy of our soul knows this too. The devil knows that a spirit of fear left unchallenged will put our faith in reverse. When that happens, instead of running to our heavenly Father for protection, we start running from our heavenly

Father. This leads to isolation, and this is precisely where the enemy wants to get us. Once isolated we become very vulnerable.

Talk to God About Everything

"Don't worry about anything; instead, pray about everything. Tell God what you need, and thank him for all he has done. Then you will experience God's peace, which exceeds anything we can understand. His peace will guard your hearts and minds as you live in Christ Jesus" (Philippians 4:6–7 NLT). Do not worry about anything. Is that really possible? God would not tell us to do something that was not possible for us to do. He did not design us to carry the weight of distractions. We were not designed as tubs to sit on our own bottoms. He wants us to trust him with all of the cares of life.

Praying is simply having a conversation with God. Having a conversation with someone means that there is a time when we talk, and there is a time when we listen. Conversation is a two-way street. There is a monologue lane and there is a dialogue lane. If I have a legitimate conversation with God, I should be able to tell you what I said to him and I should be able to tell you what he said to me. If I cannot tell you what he said to me during our conversation, then the question is, did I really have a conversation with God. Did I really pray? Have you noticed that we don't seem to have a problem talking to and listening to our fears?

The way not to worry about anything is to talk to God about everything. Since God knows all things, talking to him about everything, is not for his benefit. It is the way we release all of the things that are weighing us down. Talking to God about everything is for our benefit. There is an incredible exchange that takes place, bondage for freedom, that comes when we release all of our anxious distractions to him. The fruit of release will always be the peace of God. Remember, you will never experience the peace of God until you're at peace with God (Romans 5:1; Philippians 4:7).

"So humble yourselves under the mighty power of God, and at the right time he will lift you up in honor. *Give all your worries and cares to God, for he cares about you*" (1 Peter 5:6–7 NLT italics added). God wants you to give him all of your worries and cares. He really does care for you. It is time for all of God's children to turn loose and let go. There is power in releasing.

The Power of Releasing
There is an Upside to Every Downside

"Is the glass half empty or is it half full?" This is a proverbial phrase, generally used rhetorically to indicate that a person is either an optimist or a pessimist. It has become the litmus test to determine an individual's outlook on life. Are they optimistic about life or, are they pessimistic about life? If a person says the glass as half full, we say they are an optimist. If they say the glass is half empty, we say they are a pessimist.

What do you think when you see a glass that contains an equal amount of liquid and empty space? Can something be half empty without being half full or half full without being half empty? Maybe how we see the glass has nothing to do with us being negative or positive. How we see it is determined by how we choose to see it.

I was thinking about this half full, half empty glass expression the other day. I was being very philosophical in my analysis when this inner voice whispered, "Don't get caught up in defining the glass as being half full or half empty. Why don't you just be thankful you have a glass?" That is a classic Holy Spirit answer. The Holy Spirit always sees the upside to every downside.

Seeing the Upside to Every Downside Is A Choice

"And we know that God causes everything to work together for the good of those who love God and are called according to his purpose for them" (Romans 8:28 NLT). This scripture does not say everything that happens to us in life will be good. What it does say, is God will take everything that happens to us in life and work it together for our good, because we are the love of his life. It is not a natural response to see the good that can come out of the bad. It has to be intentional.

The first church I pastored was established in 1848. No, I was not the first pastor. The average age of my congregation was in their seventies, with several of them in their eighties and a few were in their mid-nineties. I was more like their grandson than pastor. It was a very special time in my life and in the early stages of my pastoral ministry.

Two of the ladies in the church were sisters. One was ninety-four and the other one was eighty-eight. They were delightful characters and both had a good sense of humor. They told me stories about visiting with the Indians who would ride up to the church house on horseback when they were small girls. They could tell some fascinating stories, always correcting one another in a loving way, as their story unfolded. The older sister was soft-spoken and had a very gentle spirit. I never heard her say anything negative about anyone or anything. She always saw the upside to every downside.

On one occasion, I was able to get Ms. Sarah to accept my invitation to go with a small group from our church to a foreign mission meeting. Several missionaries from around the world would be sharing their testimonies. On our way home, I noticed that Ms. Sarah was very quiet. It was around 9:00 pm, so it was way past her bed time. She was sitting quietly in the backseat nodding, trying not to fall asleep. In an attempt to help her stay awake, I began to initiate a conversation. "Ms. Sarah, you are an amazing person. I've never heard you say anything negative about anyone. I bet you have never said anything bad about the devil." There was an extended moment of silence before Ms. Sarah responded. When she did, here is what she said in her soft kind voice: "He sure is a hard worker." That was Ms. Sarah. She always chose to see the upside to every downside. By no means am I advocating that we speak well of our enemy, the devil. What I am saying is, what we choose to focus on is a personal choice. It may not be natural but it is possible to focus on the positive side of things and not on the negative side. That was the choice Ms. Sarah had made.

Two shoe salesmen were sent to a third world country to see what the market potential was for their products. One was sent to the far east side of the country and the other salesman was sent to the far west side of the country. After completing their survey, they both called in their reports. The salesman who was sent to the east side gave his report: "No one here wears shoes. There is absolutely no market for us here." The salesman who was sent to the west side called in his report: "This is amazing. No one here wears shoes, there's a huge market for us here. Send as much inventory as you possible can." Both shoe salesmen saw the same thing; no one had shoes. To one the glass was half empty, to the other one the glass was half full. One chose to see the downside of the situation and one chose to see the upside.

God Causes Everything to Work Together for Our Good and For His Glory

Reading Genesis thirty-seven through fifty is liking reading the script to a movie. In this fascinating story we see Romans 8:28 fleshed out long before it was ever written. God caused all of the bad that happened to Joseph to work together, not only for Joseph's good, but for the good of his family, and for the entire known world. It was a slow gradual thirteen-year process. Even though Joseph had many legitimate reasons to quit on life, he remained faithful and God turned his downside into an upside. God took the very thing that the enemy used in an attempt to destroy Joseph, to put him in a position where he would be able to impact the world.

God is still able to take everything that happens to us in life, work it all together for our good and for His glory. It may take some time so hang in there. Whatever you do, remain faithful. The enemy knows the upside will come, so he will do everything within his power to get you to quit during your downside experience. Your focus has to be intentional.

Dreams Can Get You into Trouble

Joseph brought a lot of trouble upon himself. He was a spoiled brat. Jacob made no bones about Joseph being his favorite, because he was the child of his old age. The scripture even tells us that Jacob loved Joseph more than his other children. His brothers saw that their father loved Joseph more than he loved them (Genesis 37:4 NKJV). The first seventeen-years of Joseph's life was all upside. Life was good for this young man. He was his father's favorite child, he was given special privileges, and he had immunity from his father's discipline. How could life get any better? You can see why he was not liked by his brothers. Joseph had a position of privilege.

"Now Joseph had a dream, and he told it to his brothers; and they hated him even more (Genesis 37:5 NKJV). It is obvious that this dream was from God, but because Joseph was an immature, self-absorbed individual, he did not handle it very well. When he shared it with his brothers and father, it was like he was saying—"in your face". The dream he had was basically saying that the day would come when Joseph would be in a position of authority. Everyone would be bowing down before him, and that included his brothers as well as his father.

Joseph's dreams of dominance over his brothers only hardened their disdain for him. Their hatred for their younger brother could not be hidden. Joseph's position of privilege was about to change, for a season. He was about to see life for the first time from the downside. All it will take is the right time, the right place, and the right opportunity. That day came.

Jacob sent Joseph to check on his brothers who were out tending the sheep. They had taken their father's sheep to graze in distant pastures. This shows just how oblivious Jacob was to the hatred that his older sons had for their youngest brother. Jacob was putting Joseph's life in danger and he did not even know it. That's how blind self-deception can be. It is hard to see the obvious when you are consumed by your own feelings and emotions.

When Joseph's brothers saw him coming from a distance, they said, "Look, this dreamer is coming" (Genesis 37:19 NKJV). If they saw him coming from a distance, how did they know it was Joseph? They recognized him by the coat of many colors he was wearing that their father had given to him. Before Joseph reached them, they had already conspired to kill him (Genesis 37:18 NKJV). Joseph's brothers stripped him of his coat and threw him into a pit. How quickly things can go from being upside to downside. This downside in Joseph's life would last for thirteen plus years.

Plans to take their brother's life was changed by some approaching Midianite slave traders. For twenty shekels of silver Joseph was on his way to Egypt, without his coat of favor. To cover their tracks, his brothers killed a goat and sprinkled Joseph's coat with its blood. They presented the coat to their father pretending they really didn't know if it was Joseph's coat or not. "We have found this. Do you know whether it is your son's tunic or not" (Genesis 37:32 NKJV)? They would not even acknowledge that Joseph was their brother. "Is this your son's coat?" They presented fabricated evidence that left their father assuming his favorite son had been killed by wild animals. This sounds just like the enemy of our souls.

Joseph's life is spiraling downwards. He was cast down into a pit and now he is being taken down to Egypt by human traffickers. Joseph's downside keeps going down. Upon arriving in Egypt, Joseph is sold to be a servant in Potiphar's house. "Now the Midianites had sold him in Egypt to Potiphar, an officer of Pharaoh and captain of the guard" (Genesis 37:36 NKJV). Being sold just like you would sell a piece of property is the depth of human degradation: He has now been sold twice.

Potiphar was the chief executioner for Pharaoh. "So Joseph found favor in his sight, and served him. Then he made him overseer of his house, and all that he had he put under his authority (Genesis 39:4 NKJV). The Lord never deserted Joseph. He was with Joseph when he was in the pit and He continues to be with him in Potiphar's house. This answers the question, where is the Lord when we are in our downside?

Potiphar's wife started making eyes at Joseph. She propositioned him on several occasions. Each time Joseph would say, "How then can I do this great wickedness, and sin against God" (Genesis 39:9 NKJV)? Here is the key to getting through our downsides in life. We must keep our eyes on the Lord. Whatever you do, do not quit during the downsides of life. One might could justify Joseph giving in to Potiphar's wife's advances. He might could use it later for leverage to get special treatment. Who knows? Not Joseph. Somehow, he knew that if he kept his eyes on the Lord and remained faithful, someday, there would be an upside to his downside. He had no idea it would take thirteen-years. God never gets in a hurry.

"But it happened about this time, when Joseph went into the house to do his work, and none of the men of the house was inside" (Genesis 39:11 NKJV). The words, "But it happened", grabs our attention and nudges us to the edge of our seats. Things are about to get interesting. "She caught him by his garment, saying, 'Lie with me.' But he left his garment in her hand, and fled and ran outside" (Genesis 39:12 NKJV). Joseph loses his second coat. His second coat would become the evidence that Potiphar's wife would use to convince her husband that Joseph tried to force himself on her. More fabricated evidence. She had his coat to prove it. What is it with Joseph and his coats?

Potiphar heard his wife's story and had Joseph thrown into prison.

When you think things cannot get worse, they do. Joseph goes from a pit, to Potiphar's house, now to prison. I am not convinced that Potiphar really believed his wife's story about being assaulted by Joseph. Potiphar was the chief executioner for Pharaoh. He made his living by killing people. It seems to me that if he really believed his wife's story about being assaulted by Joseph, he would have made sure Joseph would never have the opportunity to ever assault anyone again.

What is happening to Joseph is so unfair. He may be a seventeen-year old boy who is full of himself, but he does not deserve this kind of treatment. Where is God? He is in the same place he was when Joseph was in the pit, and he is in the same place he was in Potiphar's house. "But the Lord was with Joseph and showed him mercy, and He gave him favor in the sight of the keeper of the prison (Genesis 39:21 NKJV). God was with Joseph. He never leaves us, even when we are in the downside of life.

"The Lord was with Joseph and showed him mercy, and He gave him favor in the sight of the keeper of the prison" (Genesis 39:21 NKJV). Joseph goes from running Potiphar's house to running the jailhouse. Have you noticed that Joseph seems to become the favorite wherever he goes? It all began in his father's house.

Joseph met two men while he was in prison. Both men had been employed by Pharaoh. One was the chief baker and the other one was Pharaoh's personal cupbearer. For some reason these two had offended the king and were thrown into prison. Both men were placed under Joseph's custody. One day Joseph noticed that they were sad: "Why do you look so sad today" (Genesis 40:7 NKJV)? The cupbearer and chief baker told Joseph they both had dreams, and they were sad because there was no interpreter to tell them what their dreams meant. Joseph said to them, "Do not interpretations belong to God? Tell them to me, please" (Genesis 40:8 NKJV). What does Joseph know about dreams? Both men shared their dreams with Joseph and he interpreted their dreams for them.

Joseph told Pharaoh's personal cupbearer that in three days he would be released from prison and be restored as the king's chief cupbearer. Then Joseph said to the cupbearer, "Please remember me and do me a favor when things go well with you. Mention me to Pharaoh, so he might let me out of this place. For I was kidnapped from my homeland, the land of the Hebrews, and now I'm here in prison, but I did nothing to deserve it" (Genesis 40:14-15 NLT). Joseph is human after all: "Please remember me." This is the first time we hear Joseph say anything about how he got to his downside.

After hearing the interpretation of the cupbearer's dream, the chief baker was eager to have Joseph interpret his dream. Joseph's interpretation of the chief baker's dream was not what he was expecting or hoping for. He too would be released from prison in three days, but instead of being restored to his position as the king's chief baker, he would be killed.

What Joseph said came to pass, except for one thing. The cupbearer did not remember Joseph. "The chief butler (cupbearer) did not remember Joseph, but forgot him" (Genesis 40:23 NKJV emphasis added). It would take two full years and another dream for the cupbearer to remember Joseph. Two more years of prison life!

Now the King of Egypt has a dream. He is very disturbed by his dreams, and to make matters worse, none of his magicians or wise men could tell the king what his dream meant. Now the cupbearer remembers Joseph. Keep this in mind, it has been two full years; seven-hundred-thirty days. The cupbearer tells the king about Joseph, how he had interpreted accurately his dream and the dream of the chief baker. The next thing we know, Joseph is being told to get up, shave, and put on clean clothes. The king wants to see him immediately."

It was just another day in the downside of life for Joseph. He has no clue that he is the subject of the conversation that was going on inside the palace between the king and the cupbearer. The next thing he knows he is being transferred out of the prison. He is freshly showered, shaved, and dressed in clean clothes, and taken to the palace. He is about to meet the king to interpret his dream for him. Life for Joseph has accelerated to warp speed. After interpreting the king's dream, the next words he hears are, "I hereby put you in charge of the entire land of Egypt". Then Pharaoh removed his signet ring from his hand and placed it on Joseph's finger. He dressed him in fine linen clothing and hung a gold chain around his neck. Then he had Joseph ride in the chariot reserved for his second-in-command. And wherever Joseph went, the command was shouted, 'Kneel down! So Pharaoh put Joseph in charge of all Egypt. And Pharaoh said to him, 'I am Pharaoh, but no one will lift a hand or foot in the entire land of Egypt without your approval'" (Genesis 41:41–44 NLT). Joseph is now wearing his third coat, the true coat of favor.

Promotion can come quickly. The time of preparation for promotion is what takes time. On the way to his promotion, Joseph had to make a pit stop, then spend time in Potiphar's house, then prison, before he was ready for life in the palace. Nothing equips us better for promotion than the downside to our upside. This is why the enemy wants us to quit on our downsides, so we will never experience the promotion we are being prepared for.

Several more years pass by. The day comes when the brothers of Joseph stand before him. "Then the brothers came and threw themselves down before Joseph. 'Look, we are your slaves'" (Genesis 50:18 NLT)! This is exactly what Joseph told his brothers would happen when he was a self-centered, self-absorbed seventeen-year old boy. The day would come when his brothers would bow before him. That day has come.

Joseph is now the Prime Minister of Egypt, and he is a Jew! He did not quit on the downside. Joseph's response to his brothers reveals his perspective on life, his heart and his spirit, "You intended to harm me, but God intended it all for good. He brought me to this position so I could save the lives of many people. No, don't be afraid. I will continue to take care of you and your children" (Genesis 50:21 NLT). The truth of Romans 8:28 is being fleshed out millenniums before it was ever written. God takes everything that happens to us and works it all together for our good and for his glory.

Joseph experienced the power that comes from releasing. He released his brothers from their crime of selling him to human traffickers. He released Pharaoh's wife who falsely accused him of sexual assault. He released the cupbearer for forgetting him for two years. Joseph chose to let go of all of his rejections and hurts. That is how he was able to stay free even while he was a slave. There is power in releasing.

The Power of Releasing

Releasing Others
Actually Releases You

Several years ago, I received an e-mail that took the emotional wind out of my sails. It came from someone who is very special and dear to me. I was told that I was not wanted or needed in this person's life. It was extremely emotionally deflating. I held on to this e-mail for some time, reading it occasionally, hoping against hope that it would read differently this time: but it never did.

One day I was talking to my wife about the emotional pain I experienced every time I read the e-mail. What she said to me that day taught me a lot about releasing people. When we release others, we are actually releasing ourselves. Here is the wisdom that came from my wife during our conversation that day. "Wayne, I know this is painful for you and I wish there was something that I could do about it. If I could I sure would. When I see you hurt, it causes me to hurt. Think about this. Why don't you dispose of the e-mail? Get rid of it. Every time it's read, it reopens painful memories and robs you of your peace." I took my wife's counsel and got rid of the e-mail. When I made the choice to let it go, I experienced release. My beautiful wife is smarter and so much wiser than I am. Releasing others actually releases you.

If It Is Possible

"If it is possible, as much as depends on you, live peaceably with all men" (Romans 12:18 NKJV). This verse tells us to live peaceably with everyone—if it is possible. I am so thankful that Paul inserted the words, "if it's possible". This takes a lot of pressure off of our emotional shoulders. Sometimes being at peace with someone is just not going to happen, no matter what you do. There will be people in your life who will not allow that to happen, but as far as you are concerned, you will be more than happy to live in peace with them.

I had a lady in my church one time who would not speak to me in public or in private. When I said hello to her, she would not even acknowledge my presence. It was like I had said nothing to her at all. I was baffled because I had not been at the church long enough to have done anything to offend her. Then one day I found out that one of her daughters and my daughter did not get along. This lady was mad at me for something that I knew nothing about or could control. There was not going to be peace between us no matter what I did or said. I pastored that church for almost twenty years and I can count on one hand, and have several fingers left over, how many times this person acknowledged my presence. The words of Paul helped me immensely, "If it is possible, as much as it depends on you, live in peace with everyone" (Romans 12:18 NKJV). These words released me from taking the responsibility for making something happen that was not going to happen. If it is possible, and it may not be, be at peace with everyone.

We Want From Others What We Won't Give Them

If you have pastored churches as long as I have, there is not a whole lot that you have not heard people say. Here is one for-the-ages, "I don't attend church anymore because of people. I quit because of all the hypocrites". Sometimes they will even give the name of a person who has offended them. When people say this, they have no clue to what they are confessing. If someone has the ability to determine what I do or what I do not do, where I go or where I do not go, they have control over me; it is control that I have given to them. How insane is that? I must admit that I do get a little twisted pleasure by asking, "Do you think anyone has ever stopped going to church because of you"? It is so easy to blame others for the choices we make but we do not want them to blame us for the ones they make. If someone tells you they quit attending church because of people, they are telling you where their focus has been. Their eyes were on people and not on the Lord. If we are focused on the Lord, we will not have time to be distracted by people.

"The church is full of hypocrites". This is a classic statement from someone who is trying to justify why they no longer attend church. Well, it is. The church is full of hypocrites, but so is the grocery store, beauty shops, department stores, barber shops, movie theaters, universities, but we continue frequenting these places. If we quit going to church because it is full of hypocrites, then we need to self-isolate and stop going anywhere, because hypocrites can be found any place that we go, even in our own homes. Just in case you may feel that you are not controlled or have never been controlled by anyone, answer this question. Have you ever dodged a person in a store? When you spot them, you duck into another isle, look down to check your cell phone, start talking to someone, or head in the opposite direction. That is all I will say about that.

Here is my rendition Saint Augustine's well-known phrase that is often used in describing resentment and unforgiveness. Resentment and unforgiveness, is like drinking poison and hoping someone else dies from it. It is not going to happen. The one who suffers is the one who drinks the poison. Forgiving and releasing others is primarily for our benefit and spiritual health. Releasing others is reciprocal, it sets others free and it keeps us free.

Holding grudges is pointless and exhausting. When we hold a grudge against someone, we are constantly thinking about them and the event that caused the hurt. Our emotions stay raw and sensitive. It does not take much of a bump to cause us to relive the hurtful event. We are the ones who will suffer, not the one we refuse to release. Many times, the one we hold resentment toward does not even know it. It makes it very difficult to move on in life when we are holding on to the past. We must release in order to increase.

> "Make allowance for each other's faults, and forgive anyone who offends you. Remember, the Lord forgave you, so you must forgive others" (Colossians 3:13 NLT).

Releasing Others Does Not Change the Past—It Changes You

What really happens when we choose not to forgive or release people who have abused, used, or hurt us in some way? It tethers us to them and we become their slaves. We become attached to the very people and the hurts that we want to be free from. People we have not forgiven or released have control over us; how we feel, what we think, and sometimes, even to where we go. Forgiving and letting go of anger, resentment, grudges, and even revenge, is required for us to move forward in life. Releasing unforgiveness is a decision that is not based on feelings. If we forgive people based on how we feel, we probably will not forgive many people. Forgiving someone does not mean that you are agreeing with what they did to you. Releasing them means you have chosen not to dwell on the matter anymore; you have moved on with your life. It means you are not going to allow them to be your master any longer. Releasing those who have hurt you will not change the past, but it will change you, and empower your present. Releasing the hurts and resentments you have been holding on to just may be the best thing you can do for yourself.

As a child of God, you are a new person and you possess a new life. You will find it difficult at best if you try to live this new life while hanging on to old hurts. "Anyone who belongs to Christ has become a new person. The old life is gone; a new life has begun" (2 Corinthians 5:17 NLT)! Releasing may be difficult to do but it is not impossible. I've had people tell me that they just cannot forgive someone who has taken advantage of them, or release the pain of their past hurts. What they are really saying is, they refuse to let go. By no means am I making light of someone's pain from being abused or treated unkindly. When we refuse to release people for what they have done to us, we will continue to be victims. It is impossible for us to move forward in life when we are attached to the past.

"Brethren, I do not count myself to have apprehended; but *one thing I do, forgetting the things which are behind* and reaching forward to those things which are ahead" (Philippians 3:13 NKJV italics added). In this verse Paul wants us to understand that for us to enjoy the beautiful life that is in front of us, we must forget the ugly things which are behind us. Forget? Is that even possible? I am sure you have heard people say, or maybe you have said it yourself, "I may forgive but I will never forget". We may find it much easier to forgive someone than we do to forget what they did to us, if we do not understand what it means to forget.

"I, even I, am He who blots out your transgressions for My own sake; And *I will not remember your sins*" (Isaiah 43:25 NKJV italics added). The Prophet Isaiah tells us that when we accept God's invitation to life, He wipes away all of our sins, and He will not remember them anymore. Keep this in mind as you process what this scripture is saying. God is all-knowing. That means there is absolutely nothing that God does not know. He is omniscient. God knows everything about everything. How is it possible for him to know all-things and yet, not remember our sins?

Let's look at the word *remember* as being more than a cognition term, referring to the mental process of remembering, thinking, knowing, judging, and problem-solving, and see it as reattaching something. There have been many instances where a surgical team was able to reattach a finger or some other body part to a person who had lost it in an accident. When you received Christ as your Lord and Savior, your sins of the past, present, and future, were wiped away, and God said He would never reattach them to you ever again. Because God is all-knowing, He still knows every sin that we have ever committed, or that we will ever commit, but He has chosen not to reattach them to us again.

This helps us to understand what it means to forgive and forget. It is not that we have lost our cognitive ability to remember what someone did to us, we choose not to mention it ever again. It releases them, but more importantly, it keeps us free. Forgiving and releasing people does not change the past, it changes us. Our wounds become scars because they are healed, and our scars become our testimonies. A scar is a healed wound. No scar, no testimony. That is how we overcome the enemy of our soul, the devil. "And they overcame him (the devil) by the blood of the Lamb and by the word of their testimony, and they did not love their lives to the death" (Revelation 12:11 NKJV).

If It Sounds Good and Rhymes It Must Be Biblical

We have become very efficient at reducing scripture down into trite, one-size-fits-all, feel-good phrases. If it sounds good and rhymes, it must be biblical. When it comes to trusting God with the issues that we face in life we often hear, all you have to do to get through this, is "let go and let God"; as if it is possible for us to get in God's way if we refuse to let go of something. When people ask me where they can find the scripture, "let go and let God", I tell them that it is found in the book of first suppositions, right after the verse, "cleanliness is next to godliness". It amazes me how many people do not know that I am being facetious with my answer.

Like many familiar sayings that are bantered about today, "let go and let God", cannot be found in the scriptures. To tell someone who is going through some traumatic life experience, to just let go and let God take care of it, can add to their misery and put them under a lot of unnecessary gilt. Even though this statement would not be defined as being biblical, (found in the scriptures), it can be seen in a positive way. When we mean that we should stop trying to control our circumstances and trust God to control them, then we are on good solid ground when we say, "let go and trust God". Jesus take the wheel is a great emotional lyric for a song, but I strongly suggest that you keep your hands on the wheel at all times when driving.

You do not tell someone who is going through the grieving process of losing a child that all they need to do in order to get through this is let go and let God. How insensitive would that be? What they need from us is a hug and our presence. This shows them they are not alone. They do not need a quick-fix-it-phrase that rhymes and sounds good. Hurting people do not need a sermon-on-a-stick. They need a God with flesh on. They need for you and me to come along-side and help them stay on their emotional feet.

Telling someone to just let go and let God, when they are watching their home burn down, or their business implode, or watch their loved one take their last breath, is not being super spiritual. They do not need our "Jesus take the wheel" answers. Where is God when we are hurting? "Even when I walk through the darkest valley, I will not be afraid, for you are close beside me. Your rod and your staff protect and comfort me" (Psalms 23:4 NLT). Jesus does not give us a trite, one-size-fits-all, feel-good answer when we are hurting. Sometimes Jesus does not say a word as he walks with us through our dark moments. It is his forever presence with us that shows he cares.

Catch and Release Is More Than A Fish Saying

There was a time in my life when I was into bass fishing on a grand scale. I was not the only one either. There were a lot of men in my church who were also. They got together one day and formed a bass club. It became a huge success. Not only did it provide great fellowship for the men and boys in our church, it was used as a tool for evangelism to reach men who had an aversion to church, but loved to fish. We were able to win a lot of men to Christ through our bass club. On my fifteenth anniversary as the senior pastor of that church, my church family gave me a bass boat. I was in fish heaven.

We were surrounded by some incredible fishing lakes in East Texas. In thirty-minutes or less from where I lived, I could be parked, unloaded, and fishing on a good bass lake in any direction from my home. I would love to fish today, but I live in an area where there is not much water. The water that we are blessed to have is used primarily to irrigate crops and to take care of dairy cattle. When I moved to the Panhandle of Texas, I was told that I was now in the middle of the best fishing in the entire State. They just didn't tell me that it was five-hundred miles in each direction.

Some of the most enjoyable fishing that I have ever done has been on private lakes. I love to fish on bodies of water that are inaccessible to the public. Usually you are allowed to catch as many fish as you possibly can, but you have to release the fish you catch. That is why it's called catch and release. It is good for the fish and it is good for the fisherman. The fish are set free to enjoy their environment and the fisherman is free to fish. The faster you release the fish you catch, the more time you have to fish. This is the benefit from releasing.

I am not talking about fishing for fish. You probably know that. I am talking about the principle of catching and releasing the people and the hurts that we sustain in living life. It is impossible to go through life without getting bumped and bruised by people and their actions. It is not going to happen. What we do with these hurts, disappointments, rejections, abuses, is the same thing that we do when we fish for fish; we catch and release.

This is what Paul told the church at Corinth, "For the weapons of our warfare are not carnal but mighty in God for pulling down strongholds, casting down arguments and every high thing that exalts itself against the knowledge of God, bringing every thought into captivity to the obedience of Christ" (2 Corinthians 10:4–5 NKJV). Catch every thought and release the unhealthy ones immediately.

One sure way to live a victorious and free life is to catch every thought and release every hurt as fast as you can. Why is this so important? Because thoughts can lead to feelings, and feelings can lead to actions. The longer we hold on to unhealthy thoughts the harder it becomes to release them, and the more emotional damage we can suffer. Unreleased thoughts can lead to hurt feelings, hurt feelings can build up to resentment, and give birth to frustration, indignation, anger, malice, grudges: The list is inexhaustible. We are actually the ones who are in control of how long we hold on to our hurts and the people who have hurt us.

Being under a new covenant, the Covenant of Grace, we do not forgive in order to be forgiven. We forgive because we have been forgiven. Releasing others actually sets us free and keeps us free. "And be kind to one another, tenderhearted, forgiving one another, even as God in Christ forgave you" (Ephesians 4:32 NKJV).

The Power of Releasing

The Measure of a Gift

My granddaughter Mallory and I are so much alike it is scary. We can look at each other at times and in some intuitive way know exactly what the other one is thinking. We have had some good belly laughs together. One of our favorite things to do when we are together is to eat at one of our favorite burger places and watch people. We are people watchers. I can't tell you how many times we have looked at someone, then at each other, and be able to read each other's mind like you would read a cheap novel. We have come close to being tossed from establishments because of our outburst of laughter and tomfoolery. That may be stretching my story a little, but it is my story, so I am going to stick to it.

Jesus loved to watch people too. One day Jesus, along with his disciples, entered the Temple and took a seat close to the collection box. From where they sat, they could see what the people were putting into the cash box. Mark tells us in his gospel account of this story, that there were many rich people who dropped in large sums of money into the container. "Jesus sat down near the collection box in the Temple and watched as the crowds dropped in their money. Many rich people put in large amounts. Then a poor widow came and dropped in two small coins" (Mark 12:41–42 NLT).

Since they were *dropping* their gifts into the collection container, the large sums of money they were giving made a sound that was noticeable. You could tell by the sound of the thump when the coins hit the bottom of the box if the amount the person gave was substantial or not. I am sure the people were impressed when they heard the heavy thumps. What the people were releasing into the offering container was actually revealing their hearts and defining their motives for giving. Just in case you may not know, giving has a voice. Giving can and does speak.

What captured the attention of Jesus was the poor widow who came by and dropped in her two small coins. She dropped her gift into the collection box the same way the other people had done. Her gift made a sound just like the other gifts did. It was the sound of her gift that grabbed Jesus' attention. Calling his disciples to himself he said, "I tell you the truth, this poor widow has given more than all the others who are making contributions. For they gave a tiny part of their surplus but she, poor as she is, has given everything she had to live on" (Mark 12:43–44 NLT). Really? Her tiny gift barely made a sound when it hit the bottom of the box, and Jesus said that her gift was more than the rest of the *'big thumping'* gifts given by the rich people.

Jesus is about to define for us how you determine the size of a gift. The measure of a gift is not determined by how much a person gives. The size of a gift is determined by how much a person has left after they have given. What did the widow have left after she gave her two small coins? We are left with no doubt because Jesus tells us, she gave all she had and had nothing left. The gift that she released had a voice and Jesus heard it. We are still hearing her gift speak today. The widow's small gift was bigger than all of the other gifts that were given that day.

We Must Release for Increase

When God can trust our hearts, he will trust our hands. What we're willing to release will determine our increase. "You must each decide in your heart how much to give. And don't give reluctantly or in response to pressure. For God loves a person who gives cheerfully. And God will generously provide all you need. Then you will always have everything you need and plenty left over to share with others" (2 Corinthians 9:7–8 NLT). Giving has been and will always be a heart issue. God loves a cheerful giver. He will generously provide for them because he knows they will share with those who are in need. When we have lack in our hands, we need to take an honest look at our hearts.

Giving should be something that we do out of a happy and optimistic spirit. I have taught on this subject for many years. One day, the Lord taught the teacher what being a cheerfully giver really means. We had one of my favorite pulpit guests to come and minister in our church for a few days. As usual, my wife and I were praying about the amount that we would give, that was over-and-above our regular stewardship, as a love offering for our guest speaker. On a Monday morning, I called my wife from my office to see if the Lord had impressed her with an amount for our love gift. My wife is usually more generous than I am, so we always go with the amount the Holy Spirit reveals to her. She told me that morning what she thought the Lord had said our gift should be. It was a very generous amount, and as usual it was more than what I had in mind. I told her, "That sounds good to me". Late that afternoon, she called me back and was sobbing almost uncontrollably. I thought something bad had happened by how emotional she was. Through her trembling voice and tears I heard these words, "Wayne, the Lord told me that we need to double the amount of our love gift." Double! My first thought was, "Get behind me Satan". I know my wife and she would not say something that she didn't feel God was saying to her. I remember laughing out loud. Yes, I actually laughed out loud. There was a mixture of emotions in my laugh. I was shocked and euphoric all at the same time. In all of our years in the ministry, we had never personally given a gift that large to a guest speaker. We did this time and it was given out of a spirit of joy.

The laugh that came out of me that day brought to mind what Paul said about being a cheerful giver. That is what he is talking about. Your first response is an unforced laugh that surprises you. All kinds of emotions will explode inside of you when you give out of a cheerful heart. You are excited to be obedient, but at the same time you are also a little dumbfounded.

Sowing Determines Our Harvest

"He who sows sparingly will also reap sparingly, and he who sows bountifully will also reap bountifully" (2 Corinthians 9:6 NKJK). The amount of our harvest will be determined by how much seed we are willing to sow. If we choose to plant a little, our harvest will be small. If we choose to sow abundantly, our harvest will be abundant. What we reap is in accordance with what we sow. This principle is true in every aspect of life. God allows us to determine the measure whereby we receive.

Jesus told a story about a man who loaned money to two people. One man was loaned five-hundred pieces of silver and the other one he loaned fifty pieces of silver. When the time came for them to repay their debt, they were not able to. The moneylender forgave the debt of both men. Jesus asked his disciples which one would love the moneylender the most. Simon Peter replied, "I suppose the one for whom he canceled the larger debt" (Luke 7:43 NLT). Jesus told Peter that he was correct with his answer. Here's the point Jesus was making with this story. The measure of love from these men was in proportion with the size of their forgiveness. The man who was forgiven the most loved the most.

There is a verse in Galatians that has intrigued me for many years. "Don't be misled—you cannot mock the justice of God. You will always harvest what you plant" (Galatians 6:7 NLT). This is the law of reciprocity: you get what you give. It is that simple. There was a time when I saw this verse from only the negative side, but it also has a positive side. When we leave this verse within its' context, we are able to see both sides.

If we see the justice of God as something that is only negative, then our tendency is to see this verse in a negative light. When we understand that justice can mean impartial and just treatment, then we are able to see the positive side of what this verse is saying as well.

Mocking God is to believe that you will reap something that is different from what you sowed. It would be like planting corn seed and expecting a harvest of cotton. That would be mocking God because God established a law in the beginning of creation: seed will bear after its kind (Genesis 1:11–12 NKJV). The DNA of the harvest is in the seed. Don't be deceived in to believing something that is not true. A seed will bear after its kind. We will harvest what we plant. The truth, is we will actually harvest more than we plant. When you plant a kernel of sweet corn, you will get a stalk that will have one to two ears of corn on it. Each ear of corn will have hundreds of kernels, yielding much more than what was planted.

The context of this sowing and reaping principle is given to us, "For he who sows to his flesh will of the flesh reap corruption, [negative side] but he who sows to the Spirit will of the Spirit reap everlasting life" [positive side] (Galatians 6:8 NKJV emphasis added). This verse exposes the two sides of the sowing principle; one is negative and one is positive. If a person chooses to sow into the old sinful nature, the harvest will be decay and death. If a person chooses to sow into the Spirit, the harvest will be everlasting life. Again, we will harvest what we sow, we get what we give. God allows us to determine the measure of our receiving by our giving.

"For everything there is a season, a time for every activity under heaven. A time to be born and a time to die. *A time to plant and time to harvest*" (Ecclesiastes 3:1–2 NLT italics added). There is a season for planting and there is a season for harvesting. This is another reason why Paul told the church at Galatia not to be deceived. Just because payday does not come every Friday, does not mean there will not be a payday. We can be deceived into believing that payday will not come when we plant bad seed, when we sow into the flesh. You do not plant one day and harvest the next.

"So let's not get tired of doing what is good. At just the right time we will reap a harvest of blessing if we don't give up. Therefore, whenever we have the opportunity, we should do good to everyone— especially to those in the family of faith" (Galatians 6:9–10 NLT). The enemy of our souls will use the period of delay between our sowing and reaping to discourage us to the point of giving up. What's the use of doing good when there is no harvest to show for it? Paul tells us to keep on keeping on. A harvest of blessing will come if we will not give in or give up.

From Seed to Tree

If you have ever seen a mustard seed, you can attest to the fact of how small it is. The seeds are usually 1 to 2 millimeters in diameter [0.039 to 0.079]. I personally have never seen a seed that is smaller. Their color ranges from a yellowish white to black. It is very easy to lose or misplace a mustard seed. A small puff of air can disperse a hand full of seeds, and the chances of recovering all of the seeds are nil-next-to-none. The inherent potential in a mustard seed is staggering. Inside of this tiny seed is a large tree, so big that once it reaches its full maturity birds can roost and build their nests in it. Some can reach the height of ten feet. Don't ever underestimate the potential that resides in something that appears to be so small. A ten-foot tall tree lives inside of a tiny mustard seed.

Jesus used a mustard seed to illustrate for His disciples what the Kingdom of God is like. "The kingdom of heaven is like a mustard seed, which a man took and sowed in his field, which indeed is the least of all the seeds; but when it is grown it is greater than the herbs and becomes a tree, so that the birds of the air come and nest in its branches" (Matthew 13:31–32 NKJV). The Kingdom of God is like a mustard seed that's been planted in the ground. It began with one man, and that one man was Jesus. Jesus began calling individuals to walk with Him one by one; soon there were hundreds, then thousands, and now the number is incalculable. The Kingdom of God [harvest] was in Jesus [the seed]. Seed will bear after its' kind.

One day Jesus was teaching His disciples about forgiving people who had wronged them, even if they had to forgive them seven times in one day. This kind of forgiveness was foreign to the disciples. To forgive a person three times was going way beyond the limit, but to double it and add one: seven times—in one day! Now we understand why the disciples blurted out to Jesus to increase their faith.

Once again, Jesus used the mustard seed to illustrate faith just like He used it to illustrate the Kingdom of God. "If you have faith as a mustard seed, you can say to this mulberry tree, 'Be pulled up by the roots and be planted in the sea,' and it would obey you" (Luke 17:6 NKJV). Like a mustard seed, your faith may have the appearance of being very small, but it has the potential to do great things.

I hear people say all the time that they wish they had more faith, or they may say that they have no faith at all. Some will say, "If I just had the faith of so-in-so", and then they will name person they think is a spiritual giant. Most of these people who say they wish they had more faith are believers. When it comes to faith there are two things that you need to know. The first thing, it is not your faith. You are living life by the faith of another. The second thing, is you have the same measure of faith that every child of God has been given, even those whom you consider heroes of the faith. You either do not know what you have or you do not have confidence in what you have.

As a new creation you are living your life by the faith of another. Christ is living His life through you as you in the same way that the Father lived His life through Jesus as Jesus. "I am crucified with Christ: nevertheless I live; yet not I, but *Christ liveth in me*: and the life which I now life in the flesh *I live by the faith of the Son of God* who loved me, and gave himself for me" (Galatians 2:20 NKJV emphasis added). There are many good translations of this verse but the King James Version nails it; we live by the faith of another. We live our lives by the faith of Jesus, the Son of God. This is why Paul wrote, "When *Christ who is our life* appears then you also will appear with Him in glory" (Colossians 3:4 NKJV).

You do not need more faith you just need to use the faith that you have been given. What do we do with the scripture that says that everyone has been given a measure of faith (Romans 12:3 NKJV)? Maybe the measure of faith that God gave me is not as much as the measure of faith that you were given. The question that begs to be answered is, what is God's measure? David says in the Shepherd's Psalm, "my cup runs over" (Psalms 23:5 NKJV). There's God's measure. God doesn't fill our cup to the brim, He overflows it. When the prodigal son returned home his father put "the best robe" on his son. It wasn't just a nice robe it was the best robe. That's God's measure. The "fatted calf" was killed and prepared for the feast to celebrate the sons return home. It wasn't just any calf it was the fatted calf. There's God's measure. "Now to Him who is able to do *exceedingly abundantly above* all that we ask or think, according to the power that works in us" (Ephesians 3:20 NKJV emphasis added). This verse speaks to God's measure. When you received Jesus as your Lord and Savior, you were given His faith.

You live your new life in Christ by His faith. "Faith is the confidence that what we hope for will actually happen; it gives us assurance about things we cannot see" (Hebrews 11:1 NLT). Three things are mentioned in this verse that I find very conspicuous by their absence within the community of faith; confidence, hope, and assurance. As a child of God, you are in possession of all three because Christ is your life. Since Christ is your life, you have everything you need to rule and reign in this life.

Since Christ is our life, He is our confidence. "We are confident of all this because of our great trust in God through Christ" (2

Corinthians 3:4 NLT). Christian confidence is knowing Christ can be trusted.

Since Christ is our life, He is our hope. "For this reason I also suffer these things; nevertheless I am not ashamed for I know whom *I have believed and am persuaded* that He is able to keep what I have committed to Him unto that Day" (2 Timothy 1:12 NKJV emphasis added). Christian hope is confident expectation that God will be faithful to His promises.

Since Christ is our life, He is our assurance. "Let us draw near with a true heart *in full assurance of faith,* having our hearts sprinkled from an evil conscience and our bodies washed with pure water" (Hebrews 10:22 NKJV emphasis added). When our confidence is in Christ we are freed from doubt and uncertainty.

I read something about mustard seed that is interesting. When the seed is young and immature it appears as a small green bud. There is a period of time when the mustard seed turns brown. In this stage it looks like it is dying, but it is not, it is actually maturing. If your faith at the moment seems to be dormant, it just may be in the process of maturing. Water your faith with the truth. Jesus said that the word of God is truth (John 17:17 NKJV).

The Power of Releasing
Recognizing and Releasing Thoughts

I HEARD A STORY THAT WAS TOLD MANY YEARS AGO THAT HAS stuck with me. It was about a particular law firm in one of our big cities that gave all of their employees, turkeys for Christmas. Some of the folks who had been at the law firm for a period of time had gotten a little burned out on Christmas turkeys. By the time the firm's annual Christmas party rolled around they were making jokes and off-the-cuff comments about it being "gobbler time". This tradition had gotten a little stale and antiquated for them.

Some of the guys thought it would be fun to play a joke on one of the new attorneys. This would be his first turkey Christmas, so they wanted to make it memorable for him. The jokesters came to work prepared to pull off their prank on the day when everyone would be given their turkeys. Some of them were able to distract their new law buddy while the others removed the turkey that was in his box. The turkey was replaced with bones, feathers, and other turkey parts, as well as some objects that would give the box the weight and feel that there was a Christmas turkey inside of it. Their intent was to have a little fun at the expense of the new guy.

When quitting time came everyone grabbed their turkey box and headed home for the weekend. The pranksters could hardly wait for Monday morning to roll around so they could hear what the new guy had to say about his Christmas turkey. This was going to be funny, something that they would laugh about for a long time.

The new attorney lived in a downtown apartment with his small family, so he used public transportation to travel to and from work. After getting on the bus he sat down next to a guy who looked tired and depressed. As the conversation flowed back-and-forth between the two, the attorney heard the man's story. He was unemployed and was having difficulty finding a job, especially here at Christmas time. His family would have a very meager Christmas to say the least. The man's story touched the heart of this young attorney. In the Christmas spirit he gave this man his Christmas turkey. At least this man and his family would have something to eat for Christmas. The man was deeply move by the generosity of this stranger and thanked him over and over again as he got off the bus.

Monday morning finally came. The pranksters, were all standing around the coffee pot waiting; they couldn't wait to see their co-workers face and to hear his story. This would be a Christmas they would talk about for a long time. Unsuspecting, their co-worker walks into the coffee room at the law firm where he was greeted in unison by the jokesters. When they asked him about his weekend, he told them the story of the man who sat next to on the bus—I'll let your imagination finish this story.

For the next several weeks these young attorneys rode the commuter bus system, searching for this man in hopes of rectifying the situation and to make amends. They never found him.

Try to put yourself in the shoes of all three parties: the pranksters, the pranked, and the person who was ultimately pranked. I want you to focus on the ones who were ultimately pranked. This man, along with his family, will more than likely live the rest of their lives with the assumption that the man who gave them the box of turkey parts and foreign objects, was a cruel and sadistic person. What else could they assume? This would be their reality even though it was based on assumption.

The problem with assumption, is we believe something to be true when it is not. The chances are very good that all of us, who have lived for any length of time, are living with assumptions. We believe something that we are convinced is true when it is not. Assumption is the lowest form of knowledge. One assumption can lead to another assumption, and ultimately to a conclusion. If we are not careful our minds can make up a whole story that is only true to us. Assumptions can be very deceptive. If our thoughts are left unchallenged, we can jump to a conclusion without having any supporting evidence.

This is exactly what happened to King Saul when he heard the celebration songs the women were singing. "Now it happened" (1 Samuel 18:6 NKJV). These words bring you to the edge of your chair because you anticipate something is coming and you don't want to miss it. King Saul, David, and all of the men of war were coming home after their great victory over the Philistine army. David, just a young man, had taken out Goliath who was the Philistine's greatest warrior, and he did it with only a sling and a stone. As they approached the city the streets were filled with people, creating a festival atmosphere. The people were singing and dancing in the streets as they played their instruments. "So the women sang as they danced and said: 'Saul has slain his thousands, and David his ten thousand'" (1 Samuel 18:7 NKJV). King Saul heard what the women were singing. Thoughts of losing the kingdom to David began to creep into his head. Instead of capturing his thoughts and releasing them, so he could enjoy the celebration, he began to nurse those thoughts and they began to grow until assumption kicked in. "Then Saul was very angry, and the saying displeased him; and he said, 'They have ascribed to David ten thousands, and to me they have ascribed only thousands. Now what more *can he have but the kingdom"* (1 Samuel 18:8 NKJV emphasis added). No one had said anything about David wanting the kingdom!

Where in the world did Saul get the idea that this young man was out to replace him as king?

Saul heard the words that the ladies were singing and a spirit of jealousy planted a thought in his head; "David is after your throne and your crown". It was not the 9,000 difference that got Saul's goat, it was the attention that David was getting. David is a twenty-two-year-old young man who woke up one morning and killed a giant. He had no thoughts of becoming king. Saul should have recognized where this thought was coming from, captured it, and then released it quickly. Because he did not, one assumption led to another and ultimately to the conclusion, David is after the kingdom. Now Saul is living with a story that only he believes is true. You will never find Saul happy. "Saul became even more afraid of him, and he remained David's enemy for the rest of his life" (1 Samuel 18:29 NLT). Saul lived his entire life assuming something to be true when it was not. How sad.

How different life could have been for King Saul if he had only captured his thoughts from the very beginning. When we hear a voice in our head that is making up answers, we need to recognize where they are coming from and immediately release them. The road to living a victorious life or a defeated life, begins (and ends) between our ears. Our minds just may be the most powerful thing that we possess, because thoughts have the ability to determine what we do, who we are and what we become. "For as he thinks in his heart, so is he" (Proverbs 23:7 NKJV). The way we think determines our perspective. Our perspective will always affect our performance.

The reason a person does what they do can be traced back to what they think. Saul was constantly harassing David. He did everything within his power to take his life. Why? David had done nothing to instigate Saul's wrath toward him. Saul thought David was after his kingdom. Uncaptured, unhealthy thoughts, can and will ultimately destroy us. "Don't copy the behavior and customs of this world, but *let God transform you into a new person by changing the way you think*. Then you will learn to know God's will for you, which is good and pleasing and perfect" (Romans 12:2 NLT emphasis added). Since what we choose to think about will determine our reality, we can change our reality by changing the way we think.

Is it possible to capture our thoughts, and if it is, how do we do it? The answer to this question is found in the Book of Psalms: "Be still, and know that I am God" (Psalm 46:10 NLT). Capturing our thoughts takes what most of us have no time for—it takes time. We need to spend as much time alone with God as we possibly can. As long as we have no time to sit and have a conversation with God, our thoughts, emotions, and our feelings will dictate how we live. Our thoughts will determine what we believe and our belief will affect how we behave. What Saul chose to believe about David affected his behavior toward him for his entire life. "So Saul became David's enemy continually" (1 Samuel 18:29 NKJV).

Saul's life was one episode of misery after another. It all started with a thought that was planted by a spirit of jealously that led him to believe something that was not true. Saul became consumed with the assumption that David was after his throne. His thoughts, even though they were not true, became his reality. Saul ended up dying on his own sword. Unhealthy thoughts that remain uncaptured can only have an unhealthy ending.

In her book Switch on Your Brain, Dr. Caroline Leaf says, "As we think, we change the physical nature of our brain. As we consciously direct our thinking, we can wire out toxic patterns of thinking and replace them with healthy thoughts." That is an incredible statement. We have the ability to consciously direct our thinking, it is done deliberately and intentionally. King Saul would have benefited greatly from a few sessions with Dr. Leaf: at least he should have read her book.

The importance of capturing our thoughts cannot be overstated. God would not tell us to capture our thoughts if it was not important, or if it was not possible to do. Capturing our thoughts is done on purpose, we must do it intentionally. Spending quiet, alone-time with God, provides the opportunity for us to redirect our thinking, as well as the opportunity to capture unhealthy thoughts, and to replace them with things that are excellent and worthy of praise. Old toxic patterns of thinking can be replaced by healthy thoughts.

"And now, dear brothers and sisters, one final thing. Fix your thoughts on what is true, and honorable, and right, and pure, and lovely, and admirable. Think about things that are excellent and worthy of praise" (Philippians 4:8 NLT). "Fix your thoughts", speaks to our ability to choose to take control of the way we think and what we think. Every time I read Philippians 4:8, I think about a pastor friend of mine. Just being around Tom Malone has a calming effect on you. Tom is calm and nothing seems to rattle or offend him. He listens way more than he talks. I get the idea that Pastor Tom loves everyone and that includes those who are hard to love. He exudes a peace that is infectious. No matter how out-of-control things may appear, Tom will always see the bright side of things. My friend has learned to wire out toxic patterns of thinking by purposely choosing to think on good things.

We must never underestimate the power of a healthy thought-life. The biggest physical challenge that I have ever had to deal with in my life was my addiction to smoking cigarettes. I cannot tell you how many times I tried to quit. I would do well for a couple of hours and then I would cave. The hardest time for me was after I ate, and when I got up in the morning and was having my morning coffee. This is why I have a deep empathy for people who smoke and want to quit, but are finding it next to impossible to kick the habit.

I was fighting this smoking habit when the Lord called me into the ministry. Many times, I would hear an inner voice say to me, "Are you going to be a puffing prophet?" For a long time, I accredited that voice to the Holy Spirit, and would share that when I gave my personal testimony. I know now, that was not the voice of the Holy Spirit whispering in my ear. It was the soft whisper of the voice of the enemy of my soul. He was trying to pile guilt and condemnation on me, in an effort to cause me to give up on God's call on my life. How can God use a smoker to preach His word? He cannot and will not use a puffing prophet.

For a long time, I would hide my cigarettes while constantly lying to myself by saying, "This will be my last one", but it wasn't. All the last cigarette did was create the desire for another one. There were many times when I thought I would never be able to stop smoking. My addiction to tobacco was too great. I had no idea that the Lord was going to use this stronghold in my life to teach me about how powerful our thought-life is. You see, my thoughts were constantly centered on my smoking and that I needed to quit. My thoughts were focused on the wrong thing. I should have captured those thoughts but I did not know how. As long as I kept my thoughts on not smoking, I was only able to do what I had my mind set on—smoking.

One day the urge to smoke a cigarette was strong. For some strange reason I started talking to the Lord. The conversation went something like this: "God, I can't believe how much You love me. I haven't done anything to deserve it. Thank You Jesus, for taking my place on the cross and dying the death I deserved. I'm so thankful that death couldn't keep you and that the grave couldn't hold you. I love you so much." Those may not be the exact words that came out of my mouth that day, but they are close. What I noticed when I finished talking to God was that the desire to smoke a cigarette was gone. I remember feeling amazed and victorious. The next time the craving returned to smoke a cigarette, and it did, I did the same thing. I started talking to God. What I was doing and did not realize, I was capturing the thoughts to smoke, releasing them and refocusing my thoughts on things that were excellent and worthy of praise.

I remember the first time I went an entire day without smoking a cigarette. A whole day without tobacco! What happened? Even though I loved God with all my heart, I was struggling with an addiction to nicotine. As long as I kept my thoughts on not smoking, my thoughts were on smoking. When I began to capture these thoughts and then intentionally choosing to think on the things of God, I was victorious over the thing that had made me a victim. Deliberately choosing to set my thoughts on things above broke the power of my nicotine addiction. By no means am I trivializing addictions. The point that I am making is the power that the mind has over matter. When we think right not much really matters.

My battle with cigarettes was won over two-thousands years ago when Jesus died on the cross. When He said "it is finished", it was finished. I appropriated His victory for me over nicotine addiction well over fifty-years ago. Victory became mine when I started capturing my thoughts, releasing them, and then setting my mind on things above. No more morning coffee, devotional and a cigarette for me.

"Set your mind on things above, not on things on the earth" (Colossians 3:2 NKJV). Once again, we see that making the shift from earthly thinking to heavenly thinking is a choice. God would never tell us to do something that He won't empower us to do. It can be very difficult to be heavenly minded while we are earthly bound: difficult yes, impossible no. I am sure you have heard the saying that it is possible for us to be so heavenly minded that we are of no earthly good. That is not biblical and it is certainly not from the Lord. As a matter of fact, the opposite is true. The more heavenly minded we are, the better it is for the world.

What if King Saul had captured the thought that David was after his throne and had immediately released it? He was the only one who heard the soft whisper of the voice of jealously: "You better stay on your toes, keep your eyes on that young man. David is after your crown and he has the support of the people behind him." The thought of David ascending to the throne did not come from the singers or from any of Saul's men of war, any more than me becoming a puffing prophet came from God. The voice of the enemy will sound familiar. This is why it is called a familiar spirit.

We could play the "what if game" all day long about what life might have been like for Saul if he had only captured his thoughts and released them. That is totally hypothetical. What we do know is what actually happened to Saul, and no matter what imaginary game we play, the outcome will not be changed. Saul died on his own sword.

What we can change is our story. The following is a quote that is often attributed to C. S. Lewis. "You can't go back and change the beginning, but you can start where you are and change the ending." You and I can start where we are right now, no matter where we may be in our lives-story, and choose to capture our thoughts and begin to release them. By setting our minds on things above, we will begin to flush out those toxic patterns of thinking and replace them with healthy thoughts.

What we think today, we will live tomorrow. Since our thoughts have helped create the life we are living today, our thoughts have the power to help create the kind of life we will live tomorrow. It is interesting, to say the least, that practicing the right things follows thinking on good things in Philippians 4. We are told to think on things that are true, honorable, right, pure, lovely, admirable, and things that are excellent and worthy of praise. Then Paul says, "Keep putting into practice all you learned and received from me— everything you heard from me and saw me doing. Then the God of peace will be with you" (Philippians 4:9 NLT). Taking our thoughts captive and replacing them with healthy thinking takes practice! We do not have to die on our own sword.

The Power of Releasing
Letting go of the Past

THERE IS A CUTE LITTLE MADE-UP STORY THAT HAS CIRCULATED for years that graphically describes the difficulty of turning loose and letting go. It is so apropos for letting go of the past. A man named Jack was walking alongside a steep cliff one foggy day and accidently fell over the edge. On the way down he was able to grab hold of a branch that abruptly stopped his descent. He held on for dear life. Looking down, he could not see how far the ground was below him because of the fog. There was no way Jack could hang on to the branch forever, and there was no way he could climb back up the steep cliff. The only thing he could do was call for someone to help him. "Help! Help! Can anyone hear me? Help!"

He yelled for a long time, but no one answered his cry. At the point of exhaustion and giving up, he heard a voice. "Jack, Jack, can you hear me?" "Yes, yes! I can hear you. I'm down hear. I can't hang on for much longer." "I can see you Jack. Are you okay?" "Yes, I am, but who are you, and where are you?" "I am the Lord, Jack. I'm everywhere." "The Lord? You mean, God?" "That's Me."

"God, please, please, help me! I promise if you'll get me down from here, I'll stop sinning. I'll be a really good person. I'll serve you for the rest of my life." "Easy on the promises Jack. Let's get you down; then we'll talk. Now, here's what I want you to do Jack. Listen very carefully." "I'll do anything, God. Just tell me what I need to do." "Okay, let go of the branch Jack." "What?" "I said, let go of the branch. Just trust Me. Let go." There was a long silence. Finally, Jack yelled, "Help! Help! Is anyone else up there?" The fog finally lifted, allowing Jack to see how far he was from the bottom of the cliff. He was less than two feet from the ground.

Sounds far too familiar doesn't it? Most people want to be rescued from their past but they are reluctant to turn loose and let it go. It is difficult to live and enjoy today when we are emotionally tied to yesterday. If we refuse to let go of the past, while trying to live in the present, we will have two visions. When there are two visions, there will be *di-vision*. In order for us to live a victorious lives we must have singleness of vision.

Paul understood how important it is to let go of the past. "Brethren, I do not count myself to have apprehended; *but one thing I do, forgetting those things which are behind and reaching forward to those things which are ahead,* I press toward the goal for the prize of the upward call of God in Christ Jesus" (Philippians 3:13–14 NKJV emphasis added). Paul was consumed with one thing, forgetting the past and looking forward. He understood that for him to be able to live life to its fullest, he had to turn loose of the past. This is what he means when he says, "forgetting those things which are behind and reaching forward to those things which are ahead". Paul refused to allow his past to affect his present. When we are anchored to the past, we cannot enjoy the present, nor can we look forward to the future.

Most churches and ministries are notorious for living in the past: "You should have been here in 1953. The Spirit of the Lord was moving in a big way." "Back in the day, we had some incredible church meetings. I remember when this place was packed." On and on the conversation goes, and it is all about what happened in the past. It is true that God can use the past to make us better for the present, but when our hindsight is clearer than our foresight, we will never have much insight into what God has for us today. We need to let the good-old-days be just that, the old days, so we can start living today. Like Paul, we need to concentrate on one thing and one thing only, letting go of the past and looking forward. If we are not careful our today will be stolen by the past.

When Paul wrote to the believers who lived in Rome, he talked about the unconditional love the Father has for His children. He talked about the inextricable relationship that believers have with the Lord Jesus Christ. Paul said he was absolutely convinced that nothing can separate us from the love of God. He says neither death nor life can separate us from God; nor angels, principalities, powers, height nor depth, no created thing, will be able to separate us from the love that God has for us through Christ Jesus. I purposely left out two things that Paul also says would not separate us from God's love: things that are present and things that are future. What grabs my attention is he did not mention the past. "For I am persuaded that neither death nor life, or angels nor principalities or powers, *nor things present nor things to come*, nor height nor depth, nor any other created thing, shall be able to separate us from the love of God which is in Christ Jesus our Lord" (Romans 8:38–39 NKJV emphasis added).

It is the past the enemy of our soul uses to rob us of our new identities that we have in Christ. He knows if he can keep us hanging on to what was, we cannot enjoy what is. If we think we can hold on to the past and to the present at the same time, we will live our life in limbo: suspended between a life that was and a life that is.

Jesus addressed the impossibility of giving allegiance to two masters. "No one can serve two masters; for either he will hate the one and love the other, or else he will be loyal to the one and despise the other. You cannot serve God and mammon" (Matthew 6:24 NKJV). Do you think that when Jesus said "no one", He actually means "no one"? If a servant tries to serve two masters the time will come when they will over value one and under value the other. That is what it means to hate one master and love another master. It is impossible to hold on to worldly riches (mammon) with one hand and hold on to God with the other hand. If we try, we will begin to loosen our grip on the one we under value and tighten our grip on the one we value.

We can apply this same teaching to letting go of the past and grabbing hold of the present. As long as we try to hold on to both, we will live our life in suspension. The chances are good the past will become more important to us than today is. There is a tendency to glamorize the past, to think it was better than it really was. Someone appropriately said, "The good thing about the good old days are, they are the good old days."

Do you remember Jack, the guy who fell off the cliff and was hanging on to a branch, suspended between the top and the bottom of the cliff? He was screaming for someone to help him. He is tired and exhausted from holding on. He did not accept the help when it came because he did not want to do what the Helper told him to do: "let go". I deal with people all of the time who are crying out for help. Life for them has been placed on hold. They are stuck. Some people want help until they are told they need to let go of the past. For various reasons people find it very difficult to turn loose and let go. I am convinced it is because there is such a strong demonic influence that will do anything and everything within its' power to keep them from turning loose and letting go. It is impossible to live life to its fullest when we are hanging on to what we need to be letting go.

The best way to get free from the past is to keep moving forward. The past has no legs or future, so it cannot keep up if we choose to move forward. Before a person can walk out their divine destiny, they must first let go of their past. "Look straight ahead, and fix your eyes on what lies before you. Mark out a straight path for your feet; stay on the safe path" (Proverbs 4:25–26 NLT).

If there is anything, I love more than gardening, it is eating the fresh produce that comes out of a garden. Many years ago, I pastored a church where a good friend of mine gave me a spot of ground so I could plant a garden. This spot of ground got bigger and bigger as I tilled more ground, planted more plants and sowed more seeds. My garden had grown to the point where I was having a hard time keeping it tilled. I was given permission by my friend to use his tractor to work my garden. With his tractor, I was not only able to keep the ground plowed, I was able to expand my *farming* even more. My little spot had grown into a small truck farm. My neighbors did not mind at all because I kept them in fresh vegetables.

One day my friend came out to see how I was doing and to get a look at my ever-expanding vegetable farm. As we stood and talked, he began to chuckle. When I asked him what was so funny, he said, "Your rows are all crooked". From that day forward he called me "crooked row". Up until the day of his death, to him my nickname was "crooked row".

Why were my rows so crooked? Because when I plowed, I kept looking back to where I had been and not forward to where I was going. This is exactly what Jesus meant when He said, "Anyone who puts a hand to the plow and then looks back is not fit for the Kingdom of God" (Luke 9:62 NLT). This verse is in context of people making excuses why they cannot follow Jesus. They have their own lives to live. This statement by Jesus is also a great illustration of what happens if we choose to live life by looking through the rearview mirror. We cannot see where we are going because we are so focused on where we have been. What happens when you are constantly looking back while you are plowing? You plow crooked rows. The pattern and path of life for so many people, is crooked because their attention is fixated on what's behind them. It is hard to plow a straight row when you are always looking over your shoulders.

The writer of Ecclesiastes talks about the times and seasons of life we go through. There is a time to keep and there is a time to throw away (Ecclesiastes 3:6 NKJV). The keeping season is not that difficult for most of us. It is the throwing away season that presents us with the biggest challenge. It is possible to become an emotional hoarder and not even be aware of it. Hurts, pains, mistakes, disappointments, can accumulate over time. We may not even be aware of it until we find ourselves held hostage by them. When we make up our mind to release our past, we set ourselves free. Releasing is an act of the will and is not predicated on our feelings and emotions.

We may actually have more control over living a life of freedom from our past than we may realize. Freedom from emotional pain is just one release away. It may be a person who has used and or abused us, that we need to release. It may be an experience we need to let go, or maybe we need to release ourselves. It is sad to watch a person's present life get eaten away by their past life, one bite at a time. The best way to not be consumed by your past is to take yourself off of the menu. You do this by releasing and letting go of what is eating your lunch.

There are people who refuse to let go of their past. It is not because they cannot let go, they have made a choice not to. There is an inherent danger in not releasing and letting things go. If we choose to not let go of the past there may come a time when we cannot let go.

The writer of Hebrews emphasizes this point by using the Israelites who were led by Moses out of Egyptian bondage as an example. If we refuse to do what we know to be right, it can lead to us not being able to do what is right: our *will not* can lead to a *cannot.* "And to whom did He swear that *they would not enter* His rest, but to those who did not obey? So we see that *they could not enter* in because of unbelief" (Hebrews 3:18–19 NKJV emphasis added). The Israelites would not enter the rest that God had prepared for them, and it led to them not being able to enter God's rest. Far too many believers take the wounds and hurts of their past to the grave with them. The epitaph, "They Would Not Release Their Past", could be chiseled on the majority of headstones in our local cemeteries.

John makes this same point in his gospel account, "Although He [Jesus] had done so many signs before them, *they did not believe in Him*, that the word of Isaiah the prophet might be fulfilled, which he spoke: 'Lord, who has believed our report And to whom has the arm of the Lord been revealed?' Therefore *they could not believe*" (John 12:37–39 NKJV; emphasis added). Even though Jesus performed many signs before the people, proving He was the Son of God, there were those who would not believe in Him. Their obituary reads—*"they could not believe in Him".* Not knowing how to release the past is one thing, not willing to release the past is another.

"Do not remember the former things, Nor consider the things of old" (Isaiah 43:18 NKJV). Forgetting the past is not about us no longer being cognizant of what we have experienced, it is about not reattaching ourselves to it. It is the same concept of God not remembering our sins (Isaiah 43:25 NKJV). Since God is all-knowing, He cannot forget, therefore, He has not forgotten our sins. He chooses not to reattach them to us. To *re-member* is to reconnect something to something else; like a surgeon would reconnect a severed thumb to a hand: The physician would reattach (*re-member*) it. We intentionally do not reconnect ourselves to the former things. The word of God instructs us to not consider the past because we are drawn to what we set our thoughts on.

Life is filled with trigger events. Trigger events are those moments when something happens that causes us to react emotionally. Those moments will bring to the surface things in our past that we have not dealt with and released. We have the tendency to focus on the event that exposed our unresolved issues, and we never address the issues. When we think the problem that we are having is the problem, then we have a problem, and that is our real problem. If you are holding a cup of coffee and someone accidently or on purpose bumps your elbow, what happens? It does not take a rocket scientist to figure it out. The coffee that is inside your cup comes out. Why did coffee come out? Because your cup contains coffee.

When we find ourselves going through a trigger event, where we get our emotional elbows bumped, what comes out? Whatever we are carrying around in our lives (cup) that we have not dealt with will come splashing out. If we are still connected to our past in an unhealthy way, we will not respond to what comes out of our emotional cup, we will react to the bump we took to our elbow. That leaves all of the junk that is in our past, the hurts, pains, disappointments, loses, resentment, ad infinitum, unresolved. It is a shame so many believers live in defeat when victory over the past is just a release away.

Trigger events are like death and taxes. It is not if you die or if you pay taxes, it is when. It is not a question, if you will experience trigger events, it is a matter of when. Life is filled with hurtful moments that will give you plenty of opportunity to keep the past alive, if you have not dealt with it and let it go. The enemy of our souls knows that if he can manipulate us in to keeping an unhealthy relationship with our past alive, we will not enjoy the abundant lives that we have been given, today. God has placed the key of freedom into our hands, it is the key of releasing.

"For we do not want you to be ignorant, brethren, of our trouble which came to us in Asia: that we were burdened beyond measure, above strength, so that we despaired even of life. Yes, we had the sentence of death in ourselves, that we should not trust in ourselves but in God who raises the dead, *who delivered us* from so great a death, and *does deliver us*; in whom we trust that *He will deliver us*" (2 Corinthians 1:8–10 NKJV; emphasis added). In this passage Paul gives us insight into how comprehensive our freedom in Christ is. Pay close attention to what he said. God delivered us, He does deliver us, and He will deliver us. God freed us from the past, He keeps us free in the present, and He will make sure we are free in the future. If that will not make you shout your shouter is broken.

Jesus said to the Jews who believed in Him, if they would settle down and make their home in the word of God, they would know the truth and the truth they know, would not only set them free, the truth they know will keep them free (John 8:31–32 NKJV). Then He says, "Therefore if the Son makes you free, you shall be free indeed" (John 8:36 NKJV). To be free indeed means that we are free from our past.

I was ministering in a church that is several hours from where I live. During one of the services I noticed a man sitting on the back row. He was staring at me with a huge smile on his face. It was obvious he knew me, or at least he thought he did. I was racking my brain, "Who is this guy?" His face was glowing as if a spot light was shining on him. At one point in the service he gave me a thumbs up. I returned the gesture with a smile on my face, as I kept asking myself, "Who is this dude?" I still could not place where I had seen him, or if I had ever seen him.

After the service was over, he came up to me with his hand extended. When I reached out to shake his hand, he grabbed me with both of his arms and gave me a big bear hug; all the while saying, "Thank you so much. My life has not been the same since you took me through deliverance ministry." All of a sudden, I remembered who this guy was. When he walked into my office years before, he was a basket case. Even though he was a child of God, his past kept him bound up. He had actually gotten to the point where he did not think he could or would ever get free from his old life. After several hours of ministering the truth about his identity in Christ, he was a different guy. He was able to recognize the lies of his past life and he released them. By turning the past loose, he set himself free. Far too many Christians cannot enjoy the sunshine of today because they have chosen to stand in the shadows of yesterday.

9

The Power of Releasing
Releasing Forgiveness

DO WE FORGIVE IN ORDER TO BE FORGIVEN OR DO WE FORGIVE because we have been forgiven? If we answer this question correctly, we will find it to be incredibly liberating: not only for those who we release through forgiveness, but it will keep us free. Forgiveness is not based on our feelings. Forgiving someone is something we do. If we wait until we feel like forgiving someone, we may never forgive them.

For us to get a biblical understanding of forgiveness, we need to understand what a covenant is and which covenant we are living under today. A covenant can be simply defined this way, it is the way God relates to people. Under the old covenant, people were required to do certain things, then God would respond accordingly. An example would be, you forgive and God will forgive you. If you do not forgive, then God will not forgive you. The way God responded to people under the old covenant was based on their performance.

Under the new covenant, God does not relate to us based on what we must do, he relates to us based on what he has done. The new covenant is not established on the performance of people, it is established on the grace of God. Take the example of forgiveness again. Under the new covenant, we do not forgive in order to be forgiven, we forgive because we have been forgiven.

The confusion in distinguishing between the old covenant and the new covenant comes when we finish reading the Book of Malachi, the last book in the Old Testament, and we start reading the Gospel of Matthew, which is the first book in the New Testament. The blank page that separates The Old Testament from The New Testament even says, "The New Testament of our Lord and Savior Jesus Christ". Because we are now reading the New Testament, we assume we are reading the new covenant. We dealt with the deception of assumption in chapter seven.

For a new covenant to have a beginning, the old covenant must have an ending. That raises a natural question. When did the old covenant end and the new covenant begin? The new covenant did not begin in a manger in Bethlehem. It began on a cross in Jerusalem. It was not the birth of Jesus that inaugurated the new covenant, it was the death of Jesus.

"But when the fullness of the time had come, God sent forth His Son, born of a woman, *born under the law*" (Galatians 4:4 NKJV emphasis added). Jesus, the baby in Jerusalem's manger, was born under the law. The old covenant was still in effect when God sent His Son to the earth. God related to people based on their performance when Jesus was born. In His teaching on the mountain side Jesus said, "Don't misunderstand why I have come. I did not come to abolish the law of Moses or the writings of the prophets. No, *I came to accomplish their purpose*" (Matthew 5:17 NLT; emphasis added). The point that I want you to get, is the old covenant was still in effect when Jesus was born. God still related to humanity based on what they did.

The new covenant did not begin until Jesus died on the cross. The writer of Hebrews makes this crystal clear. "That is why he [Christ] is the one who mediates a new covenant between God and people, so that all who are called can receive the eternal inheritance God has promised them. For Christ died to set them free from the penalty of the sins they had committed under that first covenant. When someone leaves a will, it is necessary to prove that the person who made it is dead. *The will goes into effect only after the person's death. While the person is still alive, the will cannot be put into effect"* (Hebrews 9:15–17 NLT).

The new covenant (how God relates to people) did not go into effect until Jesus died. Why is this important to know? To know when the old covenant ended and the new covenant began, keeps us from mixing the two. When Jesus came to the earth, He did not come to be an addendum to the law or to fit into the law. He came to establish a brand-new covenant that is based on God's grace. No longer will God relate to us based on our performance, He relates to us based on what He did for us through His Son Jesus Christ. This way He gets all of the glory.

With this fresh on our minds, let's look at forgiveness under the old system and forgiveness under the new system. In Matthew 18, (the old covenant is still in effect) Peter comes to Jesus with a question about forgiving people. I guess he thought he would impress Jesus by answering his own question. Do I forgive my brother seven times? Seven times! A good person in Peter's day may forgive a person up to three times—but seven. Peter doubled it and added one. Jesus' response was not, "Wow, Peter! You are incredible. I'm so impressed with you. Give yourself a big pat on the back my man". Instead, Jesus blows Peter away, "I do not say to you up to seven times, but up to seventy times seven" (Matthew 18:22 NKJV). By saying seventy times seven, Jesus was not saying that we are to forgive four-hundred-ninety times. He was saying that we should always be ready to forgive, regardless of how many times it may be.

Without hesitating, Jesus tells a story to illustrate what forgiving and releasing people looks like. The story goes like this. A certain king called in all of his servants who owed him money, so they could settle their debts. One of the servants owned a debt so large that there was no way for him to repay it. The king ordered this servant to be thrown into prison, along with his wife and children, until the debt had been paid. You can imagine how devastated this servant must have been.

Falling down on his face he begged the king for mercy. "But the man fell down before his master and begged him, 'Please, be patient with me, and I will pay it all'" (Matthew 18:26 NLT). The master of this servant was moved with compassion, so he released this servant and forgave him of his debt.

This servant must have been beside himself, having a debt forgiven that he could not repay in several lifetimes. It was not long before this forgiven servant ran into a fellow servant who owned him a small amount of money. He grabbed the man by the throat and demanded that he pay what he owed. His fellow servant fell down on his knees and begged for a little more time to repay his debt. The forgiven servant showed no compassion whatsoever toward his fellow servant. He had him thrown into prison until he paid in full what he owed.

Several of the other servants witnessed what had happened, and went and told their master all that had been done. The master called in the forgiven servant. "You wicked servant! I forgave you all that debt because you begged me. Should you not also have had compassion on your fellow servant, just as I had pity on you? And his master was angry, and delivered him to the torturers until he should pay all that was due him" (Matthew 18:32–34 NKJV).

What Jesus says next is not a part of the parable. "So My heavenly Father also will do to you if each of you, from his heart, does not forgive his brother his trespasses" (Matthew18:35 NKJV).

There is absolutely no doubt that from this story, Jesus is saying that we have to forgive in order to be forgiven. The question that needs to be answered is, when did Jesus tell this story about forgiveness? It was before he died on the cross. Since Jesus had not died yet, the old covenant was still in effect (Galatians 4:4 NKJV). Under the old system, God relates to people based on what they do. We forgive, we are forgiven. If we do not forgive, we are not forgiven. Here is some good news. We are not under the old covenant any more.

In the model prayer, Jesus says that we should pray, "Forgive us our sins, as we have forgiven those who sin against us" (Matthew 6:12 NLT). In the model prayer we are told that we are forgiven in the same way that we forgive others. If we do not forgive, we will not be forgiven. The old covenant was still active when Jesus taught this. His death on the cross would change everything.

Here is what forgiveness looks like after Jesus had died on the cross and rose from the grave. "Instead, be kind to each other, tenderhearted, *forgiving one another, just as God through Christ has forgiven you*" (Ephesians 4:32 NKJV). We do not have to forgive under the new covenant in order to be forgiven; we get to forgive under grace because we have been forgiven. Because we are partakers of God's divine nature, forgiving is a part of our new creation identities (2 Peter 1:4 NKJV).

Releasing forgiveness to others is in the DNA of every child of God. It is a part of our new creation identities. We should be quick to forgive because we have been forgiven: "My sin, oh, the bliss of this glorious thought, my sin, *not in part but the whole*, is nailed to the cross, and *I bear it no more*, Praise the Lord, praise the Lord, o my soul." (Horatio G. Spafford) Do we sing this great ole hymn and not really believe it? Our sin, not in part but the whole, was nailed to the cross, and we bear it no more. When this truth gets a hold of us, we will find it so much easier to forgive and release people—including ourselves.

When introducing someone to Christ, we tell them that if they will confess the Lord Jesus Christ as their Lord and Savior, repent of their sins, and turn from their wicked ways, they will be forgiven. Their sins will be removed as far as the east is from the west and remembered no more (Psalms 103:12 NKJV). This is the unadulterated truth. Without blinking an eye, we then tell them later on in bible study, that they will have to forgive others before God will forgive them. We never see the contradiction in what we say. Should we forgive? Absolutely! Are there any consequences if we choose not to forgive? Yes! Not being forgiven is not one of them. We forgive and release people because God has forgiven and released us from our sins.

It is not possible for us to enjoy our new creation lives that we have in Christ, if we refuse to forgive and release people. The one who suffers the most from unforgiveness is the one who refuses to forgive. The person or people we do not forgive actually have control over us. They stay on our minds which produces unhealthy thoughts. Unhealthy thoughts produce unhealthy feelings, and unhealthy feelings can produce unhealthy behavior: unhealthy behavior can have consequences. Why allow someone to live rent free in your head simply because you will not forgive them. We will suffer immensely if we choose to harbor grudges and hold resentment toward people. Forgiving people will do more for us than it will do for the ones we forgive. Do not surrender the steering wheel of your mind to people you will not forgive, and let them determine what direction you go in life. It is hard for us to live free when we will not set others free.

"*God saved you by his grace when you believed*. And you can't take credit for this; *it is a gift from God*. Salvation is not a reward for the good things we have done, so none of us can boast about it" (Ephesians 2:8–9 NLT emphasis added). Salvation is a gift given to us by God when we accept His invitation to life. Salvation is a gift, so it cannot be earned.

Since forgiveness is a part of the salvation package, it too is a gift. Forgiveness cannot be earned. If it could be earned it would no longer be a gift. It would be a wage that was earned by doing something. God did not wait for us to become deserving of His forgiveness before He sent His Son to die for us. "But God demonstrates His own love toward us, in that *while we were still sinners, Christ died for us*" (Romans 5:8 NKJV; emphasis added). We were still in our sinning state when God demonstrated His love for us by sending His Son to die on the cross. We were given the gift of forgiveness even though we did not deserve or earn it.

That is exactly what forgiving someone is all about. We are giving them a gift they cannot earn and that they may never deserve. We give the gift of forgiveness to others the same way God forgave and released us. Once again, forgiveness cannot be earned because it is a gift.

If we had to forgive in order to be forgiven, a work would be involved. We would be doing something to get something: forgiving people (doing something) to be forgiven (receiving something). That was the requirement under the old covenant because God related to people based on their behavior. They would have to do something (forgive others), then God would respond to them based on what they did (forgive them). Under the old covenant, forgiveness is earned by the one forgiving.

What about salvation? When we repent of our sins and confess Jesus as our Lord and Savior, isn't that a work as well? Let's allow John 6 to give us the answer to that question. "Then they said to Him, 'What shall we do that we may work the works of God?' Jesus answered and said to them, '*This is the work of God, that you believe in* Him whom He sent" (John 6:28–29 NKJV; emphasis added). Do not read that verse too fast and miss what Jesus said about how we do the works of God. The work of God is believing in what He says. That sure simplifies things. Under the new covenant God relates to us based on what we believe, not how we behave. Under the new covenant, forgiveness is a gift that is given to us not earned by us.

"*If you confess* with your mouth the Lord Jesus and believe in your heart that God has raised Him from the dead, you will be saved. For with the heart one believes unto righteousness, and with the mouth *confession* is made unto salvation" (Romans 8:9–10 NKJV emphasis added). The word confess means, to say the same thing. Confessing Christ is simply agreeing with what God has said about us; who we were (we were sinners), and what we became when we placed our trust in him (we are saints).

"Therefore, as the elect of God holy and beloved, put on tender mercies, kindness, humility, meekness, longsuffering; bearing with one another, and *forgiving one another*, if anyone has a complaint against another; even *as Christ forgave you, so you also must do*" (Colossians 3:12–13 NKJV emphasis added). As new creations in Christ, forgiveness is now in our spiritual DNA. As His children, we are partakers of his divine nature (2 Peter 1:7 NKJV). As He (Jesus) is, so are we in this world (1 John 4:17 NKJV). God did not forgive us because He felt like it. It was an act of his will. He made the choice to forgive and release us from our old life. Our Heavenly Father is quick to forgive and release, and so should we.

It is impossible for us to live the abundant life that was given to us when we had our born from above experience with Christ, if we keep the past present by dwelling on it. Forgiving and releasing is how we keep the past, in the past. As new creations in Christ, the past is dead to us. Why give it life by thinking about it, talking about it, and rehearsing it? Many people cannot live today because they are too busy reliving yesterday.

"Forgiveness is to set a prisoner free and discover that the prisoner was you." (Lewis B. Smedes) Let that statement soak in for a moment. When we hold on to grudges, hurts, pain, or whatever from our past, we become our own hostage. By not forgiving, we chain ourselves to the very thing we are trying to escape. Releasing forgiveness will not change the past, but it will clear out the clutter of today, and create a tomorrow filled with hope.

The Book of Proverbs is called the book of wisdom or the wisdom of Solomon. Wisdom simply defined, is seeing things from God's perspective. It is not just knowing what is good, it is applying what you know is good in your daily life. When we are living out what we know is true, is when we are truly wise. How do we get wisdom? "If you need wisdom, ask our generous God, and he will give it to you. He will not rebuke you for asking" (James 1:5 NLT). We get wisdom by asking for it.

The book of wisdom gives us some clear instructions on how to release our past life and to keep it from affecting our present life. "Look straight ahead, and fix your eyes on what lies before you" (Proverbs 4:25 NLT). We remain disengaged from the past by looking forward. Looking straight ahead and focusing our vision on what is in front of us, keeps us from being distracted by what is behind us.

Back in the day, before modern farm machinery, farmers would put blinders on their plow mules and horses. Blinders were leather cups that were attached to a horse's bridle or hood that would prevent a horse from seeing behind and beside them. Leather blinders prevented the animal from becoming distracted or panicked by what they see behind them. With singleness of vision, made possible by the blinders, the plow animal now is directed by the voice of the farmer. When we set our gaze on Christ, it is like wearing spiritual blinders. We are not easily distracted by what is behind or beside us, which makes us more sensitive to the Lord's voice. The enemy is very proficient at using the past as a weapon to distract us from the present.

Releasing forgiveness is not a one-time-for-all-time event. Forgiving and releasing must be a consistent and continual attitude. One of my favorite quotes comes from a man that I highly respected, Martin Luther King, Jr—"Forgiveness is not an occasional act it is a constant attitude." The word of God says, "Let this mind be in you which was also in Christ Jesus" (Philippians 2:5 NKJV). Jesus always has forgiving and releasing on his mind.

Since we do not have the ability to change anyone, why do we fall for the lie that people have to ask for or deserve our forgiveness, before we forgive them? The only one that we have control over are ourselves. We choose to forgive and release people. Forgiving is not based on our feelings it is an act of our will. The one who really gets set free is not the person(s) we forgive, we are the ones who are set free. Forgiving, sets us free and forgiving keeps us free.

When it comes to forgiving and releasing people, and that includes ourselves as well, there may be times when we may need to say, "I surrender Lord", "I give up". Just because we give up, does not mean we are giving in. Forgiving and releasing someone who does not deserve to be forgiven, does not mean they win and we lose. That is the voice of our enemy. Forgiving and releasing is not about winning anyway, it is about being free.

When we experience hurt in life, especially when someone hurts us intentionally, it can cause us to become bitter and resentful. Once resentment takes root, our *'want to'* is affected, and we do not want to forgive. A person may not ask for our forgiveness, and they may not deserve our forgiveness, but asking and deserving forgiveness is not why we forgive.

It is not the people we refuse to forgive that causes our pain and suffering. It is the unforgiveness that we voluntarily hold on to that causes all of our grief. Unforgiveness can become very toxic and left untreated, it can metastasize to all of our emotions. The Lord has provided medication for the disease of unforgiveness. It comes in a pill, *'the gos-pill'*, with the instructions, *"take as often as needed"*. To remain spiritually healthy and free we should maintain a hair trigger when it comes to forgiveness.

The Power of Releasing
Releasing Ourselves

"I SHOULD HAVE", "I COULD HAVE", "I WOULD HAVE". SHOULD OF, could of, and would of are kissing cousins. Anyone who has lived for any length of time, has said these three things in some form or fashion. They are blank checks. We fill in the contents from our own past experiences. "I should have made a better decision when I was in that particular relationship." "I could have avoided bankruptcy if my business partner had not run out on me." "I would have made a very good branch manager if I had been given the chance." There is one thing all three of these statements have in common, they are voices of the past. Any person who has an ounce of honesty, will tell you that there are things they would probably do differently, if they had a do over. The past is the past for a reason.

Forgiving and releasing ourselves from the past, can be just as difficult as forgiving and releasing others. In some cases, it can be even harder to do. The hurts and pain that we caused to ourselves, or to others, through our actions and bad decisions, can disguise themselves as just and deserved tormenters. What we did was so bad, we deserve to be harassed by our past.

Jesus calls the enemy of our souls a thief. "The thief does not come except to steal, and to kill, and to destroy" (John 10:10 NKJV). This is the thief's job description. The devil is out to steal our joy, kill our confidence, and destroy our hope. If there is anything good that can be said about the devil, it would be that he is faithful to his job description. He is very proficient at stealing, killing and destroying. The thing that the devil is really consistent at, is using the past (something that no longer exists for a child of God) in an attempt to kill, steal, and destroy.

Our past life (life before Jesus) has no life. It actually no longer exists for a believer. That is why it is called the past. We are new creations in Christ and we possess eternal life. Eternal life has no ending (everlasting), but it has no beginning either. If there is no beginning, there can be no past. God is eternal. He has no beginning or ending, and as his children, we bear his divine nature (2 Peter 1:4 NKJV). When we say that a child of God has no past, we are not saying that there will not be any consequences that we may have to deal with, that were set in to motion from our actions before we were born from above. As new creations in Christ, we can make choices that have consequences as well. Here is the good news. We can deal with them in the light of who we are now, not who we were then.

To get an understanding of how the devil will use the past to rob us of our present life, try to picture in your mind a puppeteer, or a ventriloquist. What is their job? They give animated life to something that has no life. The puppet they are using, has no life in it whatsoever. The dummy or puppet, is nothing more than a prop for the puppeteer or ventriloquist to use to entertain an audience. Once the performance is over, the puppet is placed back into its box. There it will stay until the next performance.

The devil's tool of choice, in his intent to deceive Christians, is to use the past as his dummy. He gives animated life to something that does not have life. The sad thing about all of this is, because we do not know our identities as new creations in Christ, we assist our enemy with his performance. It is time Christians stop allowing the devil to use them as his puppets—dummies.

Forgiving and releasing is not just about what we have been set free from, it is more about who we have been set free to. When we are focused on the who we are set free to, the what we have been set free from, becomes less important. This is why Paul said that he was concerned with one thing and only one thing. That was, forgetting the past, (the life that was behind him) and reaching forward to the life that was before him. To forget does not mean the past is totally erased from our memory. To forget means we refuse to keep rehearsing the events that happened in the past. The past is something we cannot change, but when we begin to focus on Christ, the one to whom we have been set free to, the past will grow dimmer and dimmer, and the less we will focus on what we have been set free from.

To not forgive and release ourselves from the past can have devastating consequences. If we make the decision to not let ourselves off of the hook, the pain can mutate into self-loathing, which can lead to self-destructive behavior. A person's mindset can become, "Why try, I'll never get over it, so I might as well go full bore." If an individual ever reaches this stage, they can lose all restraints and do irreparable harm to themselves and to others. The thief knows this and will do everything within his power to convince us that we do not need to, or that it is impossible for us to forgive ourselves. Always remember, the devil is a liar and the father of all lies. There is no truth in him (John 8:44 NKJV).

Forgiving does not mean the devil wins. Actually, forgiving is how he is defeated. Many people will not forgive, because they feel that it will be an admission that they were wrong and the person or persons they are forgiving was right. Think about your life before you had your born from above experience. Before you accepted Christ's invitation to life, you were still in your sins. Paul says that before we were made alive in Christ, we were dead in our trespasses and sins (Ephesians 2:1 NKJV).

When you were living your life before Christ, the devil was your father (John 8:44 NKJV). He had control over you. What happened when you repented and received Jesus as your Lord and Savior?

An exchange took place. The old creation (you) was exchanged for a completely new creation (you). You became a part of the family of God. You now have a new Father. When Christ forgave you, his forgiveness released you from the enemy's control. The devil did not win when you were forgiven. He lost—you won. Forgiving ourselves or others is not about being right, it is about being free.

I am convinced that the number one obstacle that impedes most Christians from living the abundant life they have received in Christ, is not being able or willing to forgive themselves. Forgiving ourselves will not only release us from unnecessary emotional pressure, it will allow us to relax in God's presence. "Be kind to one another, tenderhearted, forgiving one another, even as God in Christ forgave you" (Ephesians 4:32 NKJV). Forgiving as God in Christ forgave us, includes forgiving ourselves.

The enemy of our soul will always dredge up the pains and hurts of the past, with the intent to robe us of the forgiven life that we have as new creations in Christ. When he tries to remind you of how bad your past life was, remind him of how good your God is. "There is therefore *now no condemnation to those* who are in Christ Jesus" (Romans 8:1 NKJV emphasis added). You will find it impossible to say now, without it being now. There is now no judgment to those who are in Christ Jesus.

A little boy visiting his grandparents was given his first slingshot. He practiced in the woods, but he could never hit his target. As he came back to grandma's back yard, he spied her pet duck. On an impulse he took aim and let fly. The stone hit, and the duck, fell dead.

The boy panicked. Desperately he hid the dead duck in the wood pile, only to look up and see his sister watching. Sally had seen it all, but she said nothing.

After lunch that day, grandma said, "Sally, let's wash the dishes;" but Sally said, "Johnny told me he wanted to help in the kitchen today. Didn't you Johnny?" And she whispered to him, "Remember the duck!" So, Johnny did the dishes.

Later, grandpa asked if the children wanted to go fishing.

Grandma said, "I'm sorry, but I need Sally to help me make supper." Sally smiled and said, "That's all taken care of. Johnny wants to do it." Again, she whispered, "Remember the duck." Johnny stayed while Sally went fishing.

After several days of Johnny doing both his chores and Sally's, finally he couldn't stand it. He confessed to grandma that he'd killed the duck.

"I know, Johnny," she said, giving him a hug. "I was standing at the window and saw the whole thing. Because I love you, I forgave you. But I wondered how long you would let Sally make a slave of you."

How long are we going to allow the devil to make slaves out of us by using the past to blackmail us with? Far too many believers are victims of his extortion. God knows every detail about the life that we lived before we accepted him as our Lord and Savior, and has forgiven and released us from every wrong that we have ever done. "So if the Son sets you free you are truly free" (John 8:36 NLT). The devil will try to use the past, that Christ has released us from, to dominate and manipulate our present so he can dictate our future. Do not allow the enemy to use the past to ruin your present life and to rob you of your future life. If we succumb to the enemy's scam, it will be impossible for us to enjoy our birthright privileges as children of God; and he is keenly aware of that.

He was a man who had to be in control. It wasn't because he was an abusive person or had evil intentions. He felt an inordinate sense of responsibility to make sure that everyone, most importantly, those within his family, were safe, protected, and well taken care of. Most people would say that he was overbearing. Being a physically large person, made his control spirit even more intimidating.

It wasn't long before he and I became good friends. We had many off-the-record conversations in his barn and at the stables where I kept my horses. Once he felt he could trust me, he began to share more personal information about his life. It wasn't long before I began to understand why he did what he did, the way he did.

When he was just a young boy, he was involved in a farming

accident that included his younger brother. He was uninjured but his brother was killed. He felt a strong sense of responsibility for his brother's death. Even though the accident had happened well over fifty years ago, he still carried around the false guilt of being responsible for his brother's death.

The majority of time he could cope with it pretty well, but there were those seasons where he would struggle. This led to longer and more in-depth conversations about God's forgiveness, and how important it is for us to forgive and release ourselves. If we do not let ourselves off of the hook, the enemy will be more than happy to use whatever happened in the past, to hold us hostage by using it against us.

This is why my friend felt he needed to be in control of everyone and everything that he was closest to. His feelings of responsibility to take care of his family and friends was over-the-top. He was their protector. He had to make sure they were safe. You did not want to appear as an imposing threat to his family. If you did, you would experience his full wrath.

This was one of the best men I have ever gotten to know. He was what I would call a man's man. It was a sad day when I preached his memorial service. My friend was never able to fully enjoy the freedom of his new creation life, simply because he could not forgive and release himself from that one event, that happened when he was just a young boy.

I should have, I could have, I would have, are the whispers from the past. If we listen to these voices long enough, it won't be long before we find ourselves being held hostage by the past. Living life is kind of like owning and driving a vehicle for a long period of time. It is impossible to drive a vehicle for many years without it getting some scratches and dents along the way. Life is like that. We live in a fallen world that is filled with hurt and pain. It is impossible to live for any length of time without getting some emotional dents and scratches. It is not if it happens, it is when it happens. Jesus said, "These things I have spoken to you, that *in Me you may have peace. In the world you will have tribulation*, but be of good cheer, I have overcome the world" (John 16:33 NKJV emphasis added).

What does a person do when they are being bombarded by these voices from the past? How do we get past the past? We remember what Jesus said in John 16, then we remind ourselves of our position, our purpose, and the process.

What is our position as a child of God? We are in the world, but more importantly, our position is in Christ. Peace cannot be found in the world, because the world cannot produce peace. The only thing the world can produce is trouble. Our peace is found in our position, which is in Christ. When the voices of the past come, and that is a given, we must remind ourselves that we are in Christ. By being in Christ, we have peace in a troubled world. Think about a boat that is in water. As long as the boat is in the water, everything is copacetic. If the water gets into the boat, we have a problem. As long as we are in Christ, we can be at peace in a world of trouble, but if the world gets into us, we have a problem. Here is the beauty of our new creation lives, we will always be in Christ! The enemy of our souls knows that, this is why he attacks our thought-life. When that happens, we need to remind ourselves of our position. We are in Christ, who is our peace. It does not matter how troubled life may get we can be at peace because we are in the Prince of Peace.

Once we remind ourselves of our position, we need to reeducate ourselves as to our purpose for being in the world. What is our purpose for being in a world that is full of trouble? Our purpose can be summed up in four words—to make God big. Whatever we do in life, we are to use it as our opportunity to put Jesus on display. When we talk about following the Lord's calling on our lives, it is natural for us to think about ministries, like preaching, being a missionary, and the like. What we need to understand, is that it does not matter what vocation we may choose in life, we are to use it as our platform to make God big.

I have many sold out, God loving, soul-winning friends, who drive trucks for a living. They tell me that they have a rolling pulpit. Every truck stop and rest station, provides them with an opportunity to share Christ. Christians may not share the same path in life, but we do share the same purpose of life, and that is to make God big. When the voices of the past begin to whisper, I should have, I could have, I would have, we need to remind ourselves of what our purpose is while we are in this world. Our purpose is to put God on display so that people can know they too can find peace in knowing Jesus Christ as their Lord and Savior.

Once we remind ourselves of our position and purpose, we engage the process. The process is capturing every thought that passes through our heads, between our ears. "For though we walk in the flesh, we do not war according to the flesh. For the weapons of our warfare are not carnal but mighty in God for pulling down strongholds, casting down arguments and every high thing that exalts itself against the knowledge of God, *bringing every thought into captivity to the obedience of Christ*" (2 Corinthians 10:3–5 NKJV; emphasis added). Once again, Paul reminds us that even though we are in the world, our battle is not with flesh and blood. Our battle is not in the physical realm, it is in the spiritual realm. The battlefield is between our ears, in our thought lives.

If we do not take our thoughts captive, there is a great possibility that our thoughts will take us captive. It does not matter how familiar the voice that we hear may be, if it does not ultimately produce peace, we need to disregard it. Even when the Holy Spirit brings correction, the fruit will always be peace. The more we practice this process of taking our thoughts captive, the more proficient we will become at it, and the more peace we will experience.

"For I will forgive their iniquity, and their sin I will remember no more" (Jeremiah 31:34 NKJV). When an all-knowing God forgives us, it means he will never hold our sins against us ever again, and he will not keep reminding us of them either. Forgiving ourselves is not about pretending that we never did anything wrong. It means that we will not keep bringing up our past in a condemning way. Forgiving ourselves means that we release what we were holding against ourselves, and we focus on moving forward with the Lord. If God is willing and ready to forgive us, then why are we so slow in forgiving and releasing ourselves?

Motivational Speak Les Brown gave this insightful word in one of his inspirational talks. "Release the need to replay a negative situation over and over again in your mind. Do not become a hostage to your past by always reviewing and reliving your mistakes. Do not remind yourself of what should have, could have, or would have been. Release it and let it go. Move on."

11

The Power of Releasing
Giving Up Without Giving In

AS YOUNG CHILDREN GROWING UP IN RURAL EAST TEXAS, WE never lacked for anything to do. We got a lot of bruises, scrapes, and cuts, but we never got bored. The majority of our time was spent outside, exploring the woods, climbing trees, jumping out of the barn loft, swimming in stock ponds, or throwing green pears at wasp nests. If it crossed our minds, we would usually give it a try. We were as happy as if we had good sense.

We boys spent a lot of time wrestling. When you got your opponent in a position where they were at the brink of submission, or when you were at the edge of defeat, you would hear these words; "Say calf rope!" This is an East Texas dialectal expression for, "I give up". Once you or your opponent said those words, that round was over and a new round would begin.

Sometimes when we were roughhousing (rowdy behavior), someone would grab your arm or you would grab their arm, and push it as high up on their back as you possibly could, applying as much pressure as possible; then you would hear these words, "Say 'uncle', and we will quit." Saying 'uncle' is an expression that is equivalent to saying, "I give up", "I surrender." Its meaning is pretty well known across the country.

When I say that maybe the best thing we can do is to say "calf rope" or "I give up", I am not suggesting that we cash in our chips and stop living life. That is not what I am talking about. I am saying that when we think we have to be in control of things, we can be setting ourselves up for a train wreck. The truth is, there are very few things in life that we have control over. Trying to be in control of everything is like trying to make sense when there is no sense. When you try to make sense out of something that has no sense, you will end of with nonsense. When you try to take control of things that you cannot control, you will end up out of control and ultimately end up being controlled.

As talented and gifted as we may be, we do not have all of the answers to life. Life is filled with uncertainties and the inexplicable. Giving up our rights to be right may be the most liberating thing we ever do. Releasing our need to be in control frees us from being controlled. It is possible to give up without giving in.

How do we release control without losing control? How do we give up without giving in? Paul helps us with the answer to this question. "Don't worry about anything; instead, pray about everything. Tell God what you need, and thank him for all he has done" (Philippians 4:6 NLT).

Do not worry about anything. Is that possible? Would God tell us to do something if it was not possible for us to do, or that he would not help us do? Of course not. Let's take the word nothing and make two words out of it. Do not worry about "*no thing*". The word of God tells us that we should not be anxious about anything. Even the word worry is an anxious word, when it is used as a verb.

The story is told of a man who was a chronic worrier. He was the kind of guy who would worry when he had nothing to worry about. Needless to say, he wasn't a whole lot of fun to be around for any length of time. His main worry was over finances; how was he going to pay his bills, his mortgage payment; would he have enough to retire on. The list was endless. One day his friends noticed that he had this infectious smile on his face. The look of peace was all over him. "What in the world has happened to you", they asked. "I no longer worry about my finances. I hired a professional worrier to do my worrying for me." "Really", they said, with their mouths gapped open. "How much are you paying this person to worry for you?" "I'm paying them one-thousand dollars a week". "How in the world are you going to pay them that much money?" The man responded, "I don't know, that's their first worry".

Instead of worrying about anything, Paul says that we should talk to God about everything. Worry left unchecked can lead to panic, and the last thing we need to do is panic. Nothing good ever happens when we get into a panic mode. This is why Paul said that the first thing we need to do is pray. Talk to God about everything, because it will keep us from becoming angst about anything.

Let me go into greater detail about what I touched on at the end of chapter two and chapter three concerning prayer: What prayer is, and what prayer is not. Praying may be the least and the last thing that most of us do as Christians. I am convinced that it is because most of us do not understand what prayer is. Praying is not about us talking to "a thing" or to some distant deity. Praying is having a conversation with our Heavenly Father. In a conversation, all parties should be given the opportunity to speak. Most of our praying consists of us doing all of the talking. If the truth be known, most of our praying is nothing more than us having a monologue to an audience of one, ourselves. We never give God the courtesy to speak. This is detrimental to us, because there is nothing that our Heavenly Father does not know. He has the answer to every question that we will ever have. It is time we start listening more than we talk.

I would imagine that most of us can remember what we said the last time we talked to the Lord. But, can we remember what he said? If we cannot, then we must be honest and ask ourselves, did we really pray? When we spend quality time in conversation with the Lord about everything, we will find that it is possible to give up without giving in, because we will recognize that there are very few things that we have control over. Prayer is not getting our will done in heaven, it is getting God's will done on earth.

It will be so much easier for us to thank him in all things when we spend time with him in conversation. Pay close attention to what I just said. We are never told to thank God for all things. That would not be possible. How can a parent be thankful for losing a child? We are told to thank God in all things. In the midst of our pain and suffering, in every circumstance that we may find ourselves in, we can choose to thank our Heavenly Father. *"Be thankful in all circumstances*, for this is God's will for you who belong to Jesus Christ" (1 Thessalonians 5:18 NLT emphasis added). Here is a quote from Eric Hoffer about counting our blessings. "The hardest arithmetic to master is that which enables us to count our blessings." Thanks giving will lead to thanks living.

The enemy is very nefarious in his attempts to get us to think that we must be in control of every aspect of our lives in order to be happy. Since he is the master of distraction, he knows that whatever consumes our mind, will eventually control our lives. It is so easy to get distracted by the things that we cannot control and not focus on the things we can control. We have little to no control over most of the things that we encounter in life. That is the way it is in a fallen world. Even though we cannot control the majority of things that happens to us in life, we can control how we respond to what happens to us. Our response is an act of our will, and there is a yes and no switch in our will. Yes, I will praise the Lord in the middle of my crisis, even though I may not feel like it. No, I will not praise the Lord in the middle of my crisis, because I do not feel like it.

The reason it is so hard for most of us to give up and not give in, is because we are not really sure that God can be trusted. To trust God, we will have to give up our need to be in control. That is difficult to do because He may not do things the way we think they need to be done. In addition to that, we are not really sure that we trust ourselves, to trust God.

Could giving up control actually be more of a love issue than a trust issue? *"Trust in the Lord with all your heart;* do not depend on your own understanding. Seek his will in all you do and he will show you which path to take"* (Proverbs 3:5–6 NLT; emphasis added). Love precedes trust. You will find it hard to trust someone that you do not love or who does not love you. It is also difficult to love someone when there is no trust in the relationship.

I am one blessed man. Not only am I married to my best friend, I am in covenant with a lady who loves me without any strings attached. There is no way I would ever be unfaithful to my wife, and it is not because I am afraid that she would take a contract out on me if I were. In all of the years that we have been married, she has never raised her voice to me one time. She has never given me the "silent treatment" or said, "talk to the hand". I have never been given the cold shoulder or been talked down to. My wife has never verbally attacked me. Never!

I have shared our marriage testimony in many conferences and have had some people look at me with suspicion. You can read their mind: "Surely he is ministerially speaking." When you don't have that kind of relationship, you are suspicious of anyone who says they do. I fully understand that. Because I know how much my wife loves me, I find it very easy and natural to trust her. That is so freeing too.

When we know how much God loves us, we do not want to do anything that would grieve him. Contrary to what so many Christians believe, God is not mad at his children. He is madly in love with his children. He will never give us the cold shoulder, or tell us to talk to the hand. The Lord will never talk down to us. When we understand that, we cannot help but love him; then we will find it easy to trust him in every area of our lives. Love precedes trust. Knowing that, makes giving up without giving in so much easier, because we know that God wants nothing but the very best for us.

Since our Heavenly Father is all knowing, he knows what we really need. The Lord does not always give us everything we want, but he will always give us what we need. I love what Ruth Bell Graham said about God not always answering her prayers. "God has not always answered my prayers. If he had, I would have married the wrong guy—several times!" Can you imagine the messes that the Lord has kept us out of by not giving us what we thought we needed? Sometimes the worst thing that can happen to us is to get what we ask for. Even though we may not get what we think we need or want, we ought to be thankful that we do not get what we deserve.

Since we do not know what today holds for us (but God does), it makes sense to put our trust and confidence in the Lord. He is the same today, that he was yesterday. He will be the same tomorrow as he is today (Hebrews 13:8 NKJV). Why wouldn't we be willing to trust someone who knows everything that we will encounter today, and also knows everything that we will face tomorrow? The reason, is because we have been let down and hurt by people we can see, people we know well, and that makes it more difficult for us to rely on and trust in someone we cannot see. Our disappointing experiences with trusting people, makes it difficult for us to place our confidence and trust in God. We know that we need to give up our need to be in control, but it is a struggle.

The word of God is eternal and unimpeachable. What the word of God was, the word of God is, and the word of God will always be. The word of God is truth. "And we know that *God causes everything* to work together for the good of *those who love God* and are called according to his purpose for them" (Romans 8:28 NLT; emphasis added). The word of God does not say that everything that happens to us in life is good. It is possible to do the right thing and have life fall in on you. You can push the right buttons, pull the right levers, and find yourself on the short-end of the stick. That is life in a fallen world. But God—can take everything, the good, the bad, and the ugly, and work it together for our good and for his glory. We have to trust him. And it will be very challenging to trust him if we do not love him.

Trusting God is one of the prominent themes in the scriptures, especially when times are difficult. Living life is filled with unexpected hardships, which makes trusting God even more crucial to our spiritual health. "Trust in the Lord with all your heart; do not depend on your own understanding. Seek his will in all you do, and he will show you which path to take" (Proverbs 3:5–6 NLT). It would serve us well if we would live in this verse until this verse begins to live in us.

It was time for my regular monthly haircut. A friend of mine had been my barber for almost twenty years. He knew how I wanted my hair cut so he would never ask me. When my turn came, I would sit down in his chair and he would start cutting. The first thing I noticed when I walked into his shop on this particular day, was that he had an extra chair and a new barber. He introduced her to me and said that she would be apprenticing in his shop for a certain period of time. Before I knew it, he asked if it would be okay for her to cut my hair. Being a local pastor, I did not want to make a bad impression by saying no. Reluctantly, I sat down in her chair. I could tell she was nervous by the questions she was asking me. To add to her tension, my friend told her that I was a local pastor and to make sure that she did a good job, because a lot of people would be judging her work come Sunday.

It did not take long for things to go from bad to worse. The first thing I heard and felt was a snip! She cut off a small piece of the top of my right ear. Oh, yes, she did. The blood began to flow and I remember it burning like you had touched my ear with a hot match. She grabbed a towel to apply pressure to the cut in an attempt to stop the flow of blood, all the while she was apologizing. Blood was all over the right side of my face and on my shirt. It hurt! My barber friend was embarrassed that this had happened and was upset with his new apprentice at the same time. After all of the chaos had subsided, my friend finished cutting my hair. In case you may be wondering, yes, I did pay for my haircut and for the plastic surgery on my ear. I am kidding about the plastic surgery.

After that experience, I found it almost impossible to relax in a barber's chair when I got my hair cut. I did not trust barbers with scissors in their hands, especially when they began trimming around my ears. This haircut anxiety lasted for several years.

Our experiences contribute immensely to our ability to trust or not to trust. When we have people that we can see and know well let us down, it adds to the difficulty of surrendering the control of our lives to the Lord, who we cannot see. Our negative experiences of failed trust, makes it difficult for us to relax in his presence. Our propensity is to go with our experience over the truth. The truth is, God is trustworthy. Whatever God is, he is completely. Since he is trustworthy, he is completely trustworthy. The more we are willing to surrender to his control, the happier and the freer we will be. Always remember this, God is already in control and he will always have the last say about everything. We do not give him control. We surrender to his control.

Sometimes what we see as a set-back is actually a set-up. In Exodus 14 we have a story of a Divine set-up. The children of Israel were trapped in a cul-de-sac. They were surrounded by the wilderness on both sides, the Red Sea was in front of them, and Pharaoh and his army of seasoned fighters were bearing down on them. There was no way for them to escape. This would be a literal dead-end for them unless God intervened. How did they get into this predicament? God led them there. It was a Divine set-up. If God does not provide a way out for them, they are toast. They are at the place where they have absolutely no control over what happens to them. When they realized they had no control over their situation, is when they found their way out. They gave up but they did not give in.

God speaks to Moses, "Tell the children of Israel to go forward" (Exodus 14:15 NKJV). Forward? They can't go forward. The Red Sea is in front of them. If God can lead you in, he can certainly lead you out. The Lord said to Moses, "Lift up your rod, and stretch out your hand over the sea and divide it. And the children of Israel shall go on dry ground through the midst of the sea" (Exodus 14:16 NKJV). The same path that God made to deliver his people, became the path of destruction for the enemy of his people. "When the people of Israel saw the mighty power that the Lord had unleashed against the Egyptians, they were filled with awe before him. They put their faith in the Lord and in his servant Moses" (Exodus 14:31 NLT). The people of Israel had no doubt where their deliverance had come from.

Wayne Kniffen

Sometimes we may find ourselves in a dead-end situation. Our circumstances may have us hemmed in and we cannot see a way out. We have nowhere to turn, but to God. God can still make a way when there is no way. Even though we may not always be aware of it, we are here today because God has made a way for us time and time again. That alone should bring quietness to our souls.

If we cannot be satisfied with what we have received in life, surely, we can be thankful for what we have escaped from in life.

Afterword

New Creation Thinking

"The mind is a terrible thing to waste". This iconic slogan, dreamt up by the advertising agency of Young and Rubicam, goes back almost five decades (1972). It was meant to promote the United Negro College fund scholarship program for black students. The slogan became a part of the national consciousness, much like "Things go better with coke".

This is more than a catchphrase it is the unadulterated truth. The mind is a terrible thing to squander. Have you ever said or heard someone say, "I would give you a piece of my mind if I did not need it all?" In other words, I would bawl you out but it would be a waste of time and energy, so I will keep what I am thinking to myself and not waste it on you.

Most people think the mind and the brain are one and the same. The mind and the brain are not the same thing. The human brain is an organ located in the head. It is the command center for the human nervous system. It receives signals from the body's sensory organs and outputs information to the muscles. The mind is so much more than that. It is located in the soul and is the seat of reason, knowledge, and understanding. It is the place of thinking and judgment, it is where feelings are interpreted. In our minds we are able to comprehend and apply perceptions. Our mind enables us to be aware of the world around us, to think, and to feel; it is the faculty of consciousness and thought.

The mind is the set of faculties including cognitive aspects such as consciousness, imagination, perception, thinking, intelligence, judgement, language and memory, as well as noncognitive aspects such as emotion and instinct.

Why is it important for us to understand the difference between the brain and the mind? As new creations in Christ we have the mind (not the brain) of the Lord Jesus Christ. As spiritual beings we have the ability to think like him and perceive things the way he does. Our emotions can be aligned with his. We have the ability to judge things the way the Lord does because we are spiritual beings temporarily housed in an earth suit (1 Corinthians 2:14–16 NKJV).

As a child of God, we are not physical beings who have a spirit. We are spiritual beings who live in a body. Regardless of how we may feel or even think at times, we are not physical beings having a temporary spiritual experience. We are spiritual beings having a temporary physical experience. This is why Jesus said we are not of this world just as he is not of this world (John 17:14–15 NKJV). How can that be? When we accepted and received Jesus as our Lord and Savior, we became new creations in Christ (2 Corinthians 5:17 NKJV). As God's new creations we carry his DNA (2 Peter 1:4 NKJV). John said, "As He is, so are we in this world" (1 John 4:17 NKJV).

"[For] 'who has known the mind of the Lord that he may instruct Him?' *But we have the mind of Christ*" (1 Corinthians 2:16 NKJV emphasis added). As new creations in Christ, we have the ability to think differently than we did before we were born from above because we now have the mind of Christ. How does this verse square with what Paul said to the believers who lived in Philippi? *"Let this mind be in you* which was also in Christ Jesus" (Philippians 2:5 NKJV emphasis added). Paul tells the believers who live in Corinth that they have the mind of Christ, but He tells the believers who live in Philippi to, *"Let the mind of Christ"* be in them. It certainly appears we have a contradiction in these two scriptures. Do we have the mind of Christ, or is there something we must do in order to get the mind of Christ? Always keep this in mind when you are reading the scriptures. When you see what appears to be a contradiction, that is exactly what you have—an appearance.

Maybe this little story will help clear up this *appearance* of contradiction for us. My first five years of formal education were spent in a country school. The school consisted of grades one through twelve. We were more like a big family than a school. Every day was like going to a school-home rather than going to a school-house. My third-grade teacher was a lady named Mrs. Vaughn. She was a great teacher and so sweet. Here is how she taught us the difference between the words *can* and *may*. If you needed to go to the restroom, you would raise your hand so you could be recognized. When Mrs. Vaughn saw your hand, she would say, "Yes" and then she would say your name. If you said, "Mrs. Vaughn, *can* I go to the restroom?", she would reply, "I don't know if you *can* or not." What she would say next has stuck with me for more than sixty-years. "Your question should be, '*May* I go to the restroom?' The word *can*, speaks to your ability to go to the restroom and the word *may*, is requesting permission to go to the restroom."

You may be scratching your head about now and wondering, how in the world does this story about *can* and *may* have to do with what Paul said in Philippians about the mind of Christ? In Paul's letter to the church at Philippi, he told the community of believers who lived there to *let* the mind of Christ be in them (Philippians 2:5 NKJV). As a new creation being you have the mind of Christ because it is a part of your new spiritual DNA, but thinking like Christ does not happen automatically. You have not forfeited your free will. You have to choose to think like Christ. This is why Paul said to *let* (give permission) this mind be in you which was also in Christ Jesus. As a child of God, you have the mind of Christ but you have a choice to use it or not use it. You have the capacity to think like Christ, but it has to be intentional. But you cannot use what you do not know you have. Far too many believers do not know they have the mind of Christ.

It is important for us to leave this scripture within its context. As you read these five verses in Philippians 2, you will see how Christ thinks about you and others. When we think the same way, and we can, we are letting the mind of Christ be in us.

Let me give you the Kniff's Knotes paraphrase of Philippians 2. "If you have any encouragement from being *partakers of Christ's divine nature,* if you are comforted by knowing you are deeply loved by him, if you know you are in full fellowship with the Spirit of God, then make my joy complete by *being like-minded* with the family of faith, because you share the same love. Be in one spirit and purpose. Do nothing out of selfish ambition or vain conceit, but in humility consider others better than yourselves. Don't look out for your own interest, always be sensitive to the interests of others. Your attitude *(mind)* should be the same as that of Christ Jesus" (Philippians 2:1–5 Kniff's Knotes Paraphrase). When we choose to flesh out Philippians 2, in essence we are letting the mind of Christ be in us. We are allowing what we have (the mind of Christ) to express itself in and through us. As a child of God, you bear your heavenly Father's DNA: You have the mind of Christ (1 Corinthians 2:16 NKJV).

Why would we end this book on The Power of Releasing talking about having the mind of Christ? The reason it is so difficult for most of us to release things is because of our faulty thinking. When we begin to discover and appropriate our birthright privileges as children of God, we will find it much easier to release the things that we need to turn loose and let go. We will discover the power that is in releasing. If we could see things the way the Lord sees things, if we could think about things the way he thinks about things, we would do a much better job at turning loose and letting go. Well—we can! If you are a child of God, you have the mind of Christ (1 Corinthians 2:16 NKJV).

There is a country and western song written by David Ball, entitled Thinkin' Problem. The song begins with these words, "Yes, I admit I've got a thinkin' problem." The majority of believers could adopt this song as their personal anthem. The reason so many Christians live defeated lives is because they have a thinking problem. Even though we are new creation beings in Christ, most of the time we do not think like new creation beings. The vast majority of believers do not know they can think differently than they did before they had their born from above experience. If we ever get to the point where we start thinking right more than we think wrong about who we are in Christ, we will start behaving right more than we behave wrong. If we start believing right, we just may find ourselves living right.

This is the heart-beat and motivation behind every book I write—identity: Knowing who we are in Christ Jesus. The church as a whole spends more time addressing behavioral issues, as if people do not know they are misbehaving, than they do teaching Christians about their identities in Christ. We have become very proficient at giving instructions on behavior modification and sin management, but it does not set people free or keep freed people free (John 8:36 NKJV). What people actually need is to get a grip on why they misbehave. It is a thinking problem. We really do not believe what the word of God says about who we are in Christ or we do not know because we have not been taught. Anyone who says they believe right but behave wrong is living in deception. Deception is dangerous because it is so deceiving.

The willingness to release and let go of things or people that need to be released, becomes much easier when we have the same attitude about life that Christ has. I have great news for you. We do and we can! It is possible because we are partakers of His Divine nature (2 Peter 1:4 NKJV). It is high time we start living up to our identities in Christ and begin to enjoy our birthright privileges. Again, it is impossible to enjoy what you do not know you have. When we begin to discover who we are in Christ and what we have in Christ, our thinking will be radically transformed. Releasing what needs to be turned loose will be so much easier

A pastor friend of mine invited me to minister at his men's retreat. Immediately I began to think and pray about what the Lord would have me minister on. At that time this book, The Power of Releasing, was only in manuscript form. It had not been published. I still had some loose ends to tie up before it was ready to be submitted to the publisher. During the writing of this book I could feel the presence and guidance of the Holy Spirit. There were times during the process of writing, the Holy Spirit would bring to mind some things I needed to release and let go. I personally experienced the power that comes from releasing things, events, and people. At this men's retreat I was able to see others experience the same freedom and relief I got when they chose to release and let go.

During the first session of this men's conference, the Holy Spirit began to stir the *secret place* in everyone there. By the third session every man shared their heart openly and freely. It was an incredible kairos moment. Men were turning loose and letting go of everything you can imagine. It was one of those moments in time that you did not want to end. I know the enemy must have been apoplectic after that service because he lost his grip on the manufactured evidence that he had used successfully on these men; some for years. I see a few of these men occasionally and they still talk about that retreat. They personally experienced the power that comes from releasing. It is very difficult to turn loose and let go of things if we continue to think like we did before we were born from above. You may have the same old brain you had before you were saved, but you have a new mind—the mind of Christ.

"And do not be conformed to this world, but be transformed by the renewing of your mind, that you may prove what is that good and acceptable and perfect will of God" (Romans 12:2, NKJV). This is one of the verses most seasoned believers can recite from memory. Being able to quote this verse and actually knowing what it means are not necessarily synonymous.

Paul emphatically makes the statement that a child of God is not to be conformed to this world; they are to be transformed. This transformation comes by the renewing of the mind. Being conformed or transformed in the way we think is a choice.

The word *form* means to mold, shape, or to fashion. The prefix *con* means *with* or *thoroughly*. When you add the prefix *con* to the word *form* you get the word *conform*. Listen to what Paul is saying. Do not allow the world to mold, shape, or form you with itself. In other words, do not let the world's pattern of thinking be what determines how you think. I am afraid the world may have more influence on the church today than the word of God. In many areas the church is now thinking, acting, looking, and living like the world. This is why I say on a regular basis, every church is not the Lord's church but the Lord has his church in every church.

Paul uses the word *form* again in this verse but this time he connects the word *trans* to it; making it *transform*. In the Greek language the word transform is made up of two words: The word *meta* and the word *morphe*. The word *meta* means to change and the word *morphe* means form. To be transformed is to go through a process that ultimately expresses itself in a different form. Think about the word metamorphosis. We use this term to describe what happens to a caterpillar once it weaves and enters a cocoon. Inside the cocoon the caterpillar goes through a process that leads to a change in form. The caterpillar is changed into a butterfly from the inside out. This is an exchange: Something became something completely different. Sounds like natures *quid pro quo* to me: A worm for a butterfly. Have you noticed that we never refer to a butterfly as a worm with wings, yet we will identify a child of God as a sinner saved by grace? To me, that is the same thing as referring to a butterfly as a worm with wings. Even though we are new creations in Christ, we still live in the same old bodies we were born with. Our problem is not that we still have the same old bodies, our problem is we still think like worms. We have a *thinkin' problem*. This *thinkin' problem* can be overcome when we *let* the mind of Christ express itself through us. "Let (allow) this mind be in you which was also in Christ Jesus" (Philippians 2:5 NKJV). As a new creation you have the mind of Christ.

This transformation comes from the renewing of our minds. Renewing our minds is not about adding copious amounts of information to the files we maintain in our heads. That is knowledge. Renewing our minds is about intimacy (knowing) with Jesus in our hearts (mind). Paul is not talking about intellectual knowledge he is talking about experiential knowledge. It is the difference between knowing about the Lord and knowing him. This is exactly why Jesus said, "If you abide in my word, you are My disciples indeed and you shall know the truth, and the truth shall make you free" (John 8:31–32 NKJV). When we settle down and make our home in the written word of God (which is truth), we shall know the truth and the truth we know will not only make us free, the truth of God will keep us free. John did not say that truth will set us free. Truth is truth rather we are free or not. He said the truth we know, the truth we are intimate with, sets us free. As we come to know him more and more our minds will be continuously renewed. The Lord allows us to set the measurement for how much we receive. He still fills the hearts of the hungry with good things (Luke 1:53 NKJV). The question is, how hungry are you to know who you are in Christ? When you begin to think about yourself the way the Lord thinks about you, when you see things from his perspective, life becomes freer and more enjoyable

"That *you may prove* what is that good and acceptable and perfect will of God" (Romans 12:2 NKJV emphasis added). To prove means to demonstrate or to show. If there is anything the world needs to see demonstrated is that God is real, and the life he gives is unmatched by anything the world has to offer. Can you imagine the difference and the impact Christians would have on this world if we fleshed out our new creation life? I have good news for you beloved. There is an incredible awakening all around the world. Believers who are hungry are getting a revelation of their new creation identity. Their minds are being renewed because they are discovering that Christ is not just a part of their life, Christ is their life (Colossians 3:4 NKJV).

"Beloved, *now* we are children of God; and it has not yet been revealed what we shall be, but we know that when He is revealed, *we shall be like Him*, for we shall see Him as He is" (1 John 3:2 NKJV emphasis added). Being a child of God is not a future event for those who have accepted and received Jesus Christ as their Lord and Savior. You became a child of God the moment you said yes to his invitation to life, and you will be his child throughout eternity. But much of what we will experience in the future has not been revealed to us yet. We will be given new glorified bodies and we will be in God's presence forever, in a way that is far beyond anything we can comprehend while living in this natural realm. There are certain things that will not be revealed to us until Jesus comes to take us out of this earthly domain. When that happens, John says we will see God *"as He is"* and we will see that we are just like Him. "As He is, *so are we* in this world" (1 John 4:17 NKJV emphasis added). We will not be like Him some day. We are like Him today.

The mind of Christ that we were given on our spiritual birth date is a terrible thing to squander. As a child of God, you have the mind of Christ. It is time we discover what our birthright privileges are and start making God big to a lost and dying world. It is time to turn loose of the old way of thinking and let the mind of Christ express itself in and through us. There is power in releasing.

Prayer of Releasing

Releasing and letting go of anything can be difficult for most people, because we have a proclivity to think that we must be in control, or need to be. We end up being controlled by the very thing we are trying to control. With help from the Holy Spirit, we can turn loose and let go. Once we do, we will discover the power of releasing. The freedom we all long for, is found in releasing our need to be in control to God. The power of releasing is just one prayer away.

> "Trust in the Lord with all your heart; do not depend on your own understanding. Seek his will in all you do, and he will show you which path to take" (Proverbs 3:5–6 NLT).

Heavenly Father—

Thank you for loving me the way you do, and for making me complete. In you, I lack absolutely nothing. Thank you for not only forgiving and releasing me from all of my past sins, but from my present sins, as well as from all of my future sins. You have given me your promise, that you will never reattach them to me again. You have removed them as far as the east is from the west.

As you chose to forgive and release me, I choose to forgive and release everyone who has hurt me, took advantage of me, abused me, rejected me, lied about me, spoke against me, overlooked me, abandoned me, and those who did not love me when I desperately needed to be loved.

I forgive and release myself from all of the bad choices I have made: For all the times when I knew you were my answer, but chose not to turn to you. I forgive and release myself for not living up to the promises that I have made to you, when I bargained for your help and assistance during times of crisis. I forgive and release myself from all of the bad decisions I have made in my attempt to control my situation; for the times I failed and did not lived up to who I am in Christ. I release right now, my need to be in control of any and everything.

In You I live, move and have my being. You are my life. You have set me free and I am free indeed!

Name: _____

I prayed this prayer of release on: _____

Prayer to Receive Jesus Christ as Your Personal Lord and Savior

Maybe you have never accepted and received Jesus Christ as your personal Lord and Savior, or you are not sure it is well with your soul. This decision will determine where you will spend eternity. After death there will be no *do-overs*. Time is not refundable. Do not gamble with something that has eternal significance. Someday we will stand before Him as our loving Heavenly Father, or as our Holy and Righteous Judge. The decision you make now will determine which one you stand before. The ball is in your court. Heaven is waiting on you.

If you are not sure that you have had a born-from-above experience, the following prayer of salvation is for you. The Lord has told us what to do to have the assurance we will spend eternity with Him. If we do what He tells us to do, can we trust Him to do what He said He would do? It all boils down to, "Can we trust God"? The answer is an unequivocal, yes! God cannot lie.

> "If you confess with your mouth the Lord Jesus and believe in your heart that God raised Him from the dead, you will be saved. For with the heart one believes unto righteousness, and with the mouth confession is made unto salvation. For whoever calls on the name of the Lord shall be saved" (Romans 10:9–13, NKJV).

Heavenly Father —

I am accepting Your invitation to a new life. I want to live the rest of my life here on the earth with absolute settled confidence, that I will spend eternity with You when I die. I know I am a sinner and I ask for Your forgiveness. I confess with my mouth that Jesus Christ is the Son of God. I believe in my heart that Jesus died for my sins, and that you raised Him from the dead. I give you my old life and in exchange, I receive my new creation life. By faith, I receive Jesus Christ as my Lord and as my Savior. Thank you for hearing my prayer and for saving my soul.

If you prayed this prayer, I want to welcome you into the Family of God.

Name: _____
I accepted and received Jesus Christ as my Lord and Savior on: _____

About the Author

Wayne and his beloved wife, Betty Ann, (now in the presence of the Lord) live in the panhandle of Texas, where he serves as senior pastor of a local church. Kniffen has been a pastor for almost fifty-years. He has become a prolific writer in this last season of his life.

Kniffen is known for his quick wit and ability to make people laugh. One of his *Kniffenisms* is—"People will swallow more truth if they can laugh it down." It has been said that Wayne has the ability to take the simply profound and make it profoundly simple.

Over the years Wayne has been passionate about many things. Once something captures his attention and interest, he is all in. At one time he was an avid golfer, runner, horse trainer, fisherman, and hunter. Because of physical limitations and age, his passion as turned to writing. He is committed to doing what he feels the Lord has assigned him to do in his last season—and that is to make sure that what he leaves will live on. This has been his motivation for writing. The burning desire of his heart is for Christians to get a revelation of their new creation identities. What he has penned will bring inspiration, hope, and encouragement to people long after he is gone.

For personal contact:
waynekniffen@outlook.com

Printed in the United States
by Baker & Taylor Publisher Services